WELFARE CHEESE
to
FINE CAVIAR

WELFARE CHEESE
to
FINE CAVIAR

THOMAS WIDEMAN MBA, PMP

A GIFT FOR YOU!

Download the companion guide to this book today and track your progress.

www.welfarecheesetofinecaviar.com/free

Don't Wait!

Copyright © 2021 by Thomas Wideman
All rights reserved. This book or any portion thereof
may not be reproduced or used in any manner whatsoever
without the express written permission of the publisher
except for the use of brief quotations in a book review.

Cover design by Kristen Ingebretson
Interior layout and design by KUHN Design Group (kuhndesigngroup.com)
Developmental Editing by Trelani Michelle (www.Sofundamental.com)
and Nicole Harp (www.CocoStudio.com)
Copyediting and Proofread by Lana Barnes and Abbey Espinoza

First Published in May 2021

978-1-7364630-0-0 (paperback)
978-1-7364630-1-7 (ebook)
Library of Congress Control Number: 2021903100

Signs of Care Publishing
3595 Canton Road
Suite 312-149
Marietta, GA 30066

Printed in the United States of America on acid-free paper.

www.WelfareCheesetoFineCaviar.com

If you would like more information about authorizations,
speaking engagements and other products and services,
please visit our website or write publisher above.

Unless otherwise indicated, all Scripture quotations
are taking from King James Version (KJV)

I have tried to recreate events, locales and conversations from my memories of them. In order to maintain their anonymity in some instances I have changed the names of individuals and places, I may have changed some identifying characteristics and details such as physical properties, occupations and places of residence.

Although the author and publisher have made every effort to ensure that the information in this book was correct at press time, the author and publisher do not assume and hereby disclaim any liability to any party for any loss, damage, or disruption caused by errors or omissions, whether such errors or omissions result from negligence, accident, or any other cause.

ACKNOWLEDGMENTS

To Melanie: You are my inspiration and the reason that I work as hard as I do. You are so talented and beautiful. Keep striving for your dreams.

To Isaiah and Noah: You constantly amaze me. It provides me great pleasure watching you grow into strong, intelligent young men.

To the late Rosa Mae Parks Wideman (Grandma): I would not be where I am today without you. Thank you!

To my mother: Now that I have children of my own, I understand what you protected me from during my youth. Thank you.

To my brother Mike: You have the best memory. Thank you for everything you have done for the family and me. You have always been in my corner.

To Kendall Minor and Ernie S.: Thank you for always picking me up when I was down, helping me understand my true value, and getting me back in the gym.

To Aunt Barbara and Cousin Valerie: Thank you for the money, reassurance, and other support during college. When I wanted to give up, you kept pushing me.

To Ronald Dunham (Dee), Rico Chancellor, James Fant, Art Barnwell, Allen Thomason (Dude), Rodney W., Andre W. (brother), Ronseur W. (brother) and Thomas B. (Mimi): You have been the best brothers I could have ever hoped for. You helped me grow to new levels and delivered meaning and encouragement during my down times.

To James and Jkeonye M. and Norris and Rozena D.: Can you believe that we have vacationed together for nineteen years? The destinations have been great. But the conversations have been priceless. We have grown so much together. Go Gamecocks!!!

To Darryl Wall: You have been a great mentor and friend throughout my career. Your constructive feedback and encouragement have been invaluable.

To Nicole (CocoStudio.com) and Trelani (Sofundamental.com): You helped me organize my thoughts and tell my story in a way that makes sense to the readers. Your services were priceless.

To Lana Barnes and Abbey Espinoza: Your attention to detail was spectacular. Thank you for helping me with my whos and thats.

To Ed W. (my barber): Your listening ear and spiritual counsel over the last twenty years has been greatly appreciated. I do not always respond but I am thinking about every word.

To Kennedy T., Deanna M, ChiQuita G., Kellee N., Tina R., Alicia W. and Terri S.: You are the best work family. Thank you for helping me to laugh and relax more.

To Tracy U., Robert S., Carl M., Mike M., Asa H., Ed H., Ned W., Charles R., Charlie B., Royce B., and the many other adopted uncles on the job: You opened your hearts, minds, homes, and mouths to help me avoid pitfalls as I grew professionally.

To my readers, coworkers, family, teachers, classmates, professors, and friends: Thank you for allowing me to stand on your shoulders! Success is never achieved alone.

To the hardworking, selfless readers who continue to smile regardless of their current situation and press forward every day making this country a better place. I see and admire you! This book contains a few nuggets that I wish I had sooner in my journey.

Contents

Preface 13

Father, Where Are You Taking Me? 17
From Welfare Cheese 21
Poor No More 27
Peer Pressure and Race 41
The Thomas Special 53
The Death of a Role Model 61
I Am Never Getting Married 71
Control Your Response 85
The Payoff 97
Life is Short. Live it Well. 113
Sharpen Your Focus 125
Loss 135
   Who Is That Strong Woman 138
Fine Caviar 145
Final Thoughts 153
Until We Meet Again 161

Bibliography 163
Other Great Books In My Library 165
Having Fun Writing (Unedited) 167

PREFACE

I never envisioned that "Father, Where Are You Taking Me," my first speech for Toastmasters International,* would lead to the birth of this book. In 2000, I joined a club at my church, Gospel Water Branch Baptist, in Augusta, Georgia. For those of you who are unfamiliar with the Toastmasters organization, your first speech is about yourself. The club members, including my pastor at the time, loved the speech so much that I was invited to present it to the congregation on Father's Day. I received a standing ovation for a speech that I had prayed a couple of weeks for inspiration to write, only to be given it the night before its due date.

I wrote the first version of this book in 2004, paid thousands of dollars to have it professionally edited, and then put the final manuscript in a box because of fear. I did not want people, especially at my job, to know about my upbringing. Already dealing with and overcoming false stereotypes, I did not want to take a step backward. Crazy as this sounds, I am glad that I placed the manuscript in that box.

---

* Toastmasters International is an educational organization that operates clubs worldwide for the purpose of promoting communication, public speaking, and leadership. https://toastmasters.org/

I was a different person then. I had overcome a lot and felt that I could handle anything. In hindsight, I didn't understand as much as I thought I did. Having married Melanie in 2001, I was still in the honeymoon stages of my marriage, my career, my faith, and my life. Isaiah, our oldest son, was not born until 2005, and Noah followed in 2008.

It was astounding how raising children, dealing with rough patches in my marriage, recovering from career setbacks, facing personal financial challenges, and overcoming my ego changed my view on life. And when I thought I had reached the pinnacle of success, my wife resigned from her high-paying job to pursue her dreams of building a bakery business from home. The death of my grandmother, one of the strongest women on this earth, further shaped my views. Shortly thereafter, I faced another career setback at a time when my clients and I had felt that I was exceeding all expectations. Surrounded by uncertainty, my wife and I decided to take her dream to the next level by acquiring a small bakery in Decatur, Georgia, in January 2019.

And then the year that will forever live in everyone's mind arrived, 2020 (including January 2021). The global pandemic, social unrest, extreme political divisions—just to name a few—were the turning points for this book's release. The fact that I could leave my home and not return, or that my family and I could be infected by the virus and not recover, weighed on me.

In this book, I have opened my closet of uncomfortable experiences (some that have been tucked away in a locked box for decades) to share with you, in hopes that I can help you understand a different perspective, expand your comfort zone, and provide an ingredient for succeeding in your dreams. To protect the identities of people mentioned in the book, I have changed their names.

In closing, you are a beautiful creation of God. I wish you much success in your endeavors and challenge you to expand your comfort zone. Show empathy to others and help improve society one person at a time.

Father, Where Are You Taking Me?

Dear Father, where are You taking me?
You started me out in a single-parent home with
three younger brothers. Each of my brothers
had a different dad. Where was mine?
I was three years old when you let me see him last.
My brothers received gifts and money from their
dads. I received nothing, not even child support.
I later discovered that my dad was a murderer.
He killed his wife on the steps of Your House.
I appreciate You getting my dad away from my mom.
Father, where are You taking me?

You allowed my life to be a struggle from
the very beginning. As a child, other kids
picked on me because of my eyes.
They called me "cross-eyed," "Cyclops," "Dead Eye," and
other names that established a permanent emotional scar.
Even today, some people think that I am looking at
others when I am talking to them. But even with this
cosmetic flaw, You blessed me with Melanie, one of
the most beautiful, supportive wives in the world.
Father, where are You taking me?

You made me an outcast by terming me "gifted."
You took me out of classes with my friends and
placed me in ones where I did not fit in.
I did not have parents with professions.
My mom could not help me with my homework.
No one in my apartment complex could help me either.
In fact, my mom could not afford to send me on field
trips or pay for school lunch, much less college.
However, You always appeared through
someone or something…
Whether it was welfare, food stamps, free lunch,
student loans, scholarships, or generous people.
Father, where are You taking me?

You taught me about drugs early in my life.
You let me see them, touch them, and hold them.
You also showed me the effect of drugs.
My friends that were dealers had money, cars, jewelry, etc.
And when I considered giving up and becoming
a dealer, You introduced the real impact
of drugs when it mattered the most.
And oh, how I remember watching my grandmother,
one of the strongest women on this earth, cry for
her son who would break into the house, steal
things, and then run off into the night.
And when I thought that was the end of the lesson…
My best friend, whom I claimed as my older
brother, lost his life at the hands of another
so-called friend of ours because of the stuff.
But You always gave me the strength
to avoid using or selling them.
Father, where are You taking me?

You placed me in positions where I was in the spotlight.
In elementary school, You allowed me to sing at the
World's Fair in New Orleans, win two school spelling bees,
and attend special weekly regional brainstorming classes.
In high school, You made me student body vice president,
the starting cornerback on the football team, and a
student liaison for the Parent Teacher Association.
In college, you allowed me to attend a semester
at North Carolina State University through the
National Student Exchange Program, work a
summer in Texas as an Inroads intern with Union
Carbide Corporation, and attend conferences
in Baltimore, Greensboro, and Anaheim.
Father, where are You taking me?

You placed dreams in my head at night of
being a leader, but you never told me of what,
where, and whom I was going to lead.
You place me in leadership positions often.
However, You never tell me why.
According to my old boss, I earn more money
than 80 percent of the population.
But You guided me to budget every penny
to pay off debt and live for the future.
Father, where are You taking me?

You have given me high expectations for
myself and for those close to me.
And everyone, except my grandmother, has let me down.
But I still love them all.
When my head is in the clouds,
You knock me down to earth quickly.
When my back is against the ground, You raise me slowly.
But You are always there.
Father, where are You taking me?

I know there are others like me out there.
And I want to help show them the way.
But You continuously tell me that I am not ready yet.
Father, where are You taking me?
Father, please answer my prayers, so that
I may live Your will to the utmost.

Amen.

From Welfare Cheese

*Saving for a rainy day is tough
when you live in a rainforest.*

My life is a picture of success. I can say that I am living the American Dream. I am not rich by any means, at least not yet. But I have visited more than eleven international cities, including Paris, France. I have vacationed at lavish resorts. I have eaten at five-star restaurants. And I have flown first-class on both domestic and international flights.

Zoom in to see family. I have a beautiful wife and two healthy sons ages fifteen and twelve. We live in a four-bedroom, three-bathroom home with two kitchens in a quiet but diverse neighborhood—except for my neighbor, who plays loud music on his vehicle's speakers. I am not complaining because I love loud music as well, just not at 11:00 p.m. on a work night.

Zoom out to see education and career. I have two degrees: a Bachelor of Science in Chemical Engineering from the University of South Carolina, and a Master of Business Administration with a focus in Finance from Georgia State University—both respected universities. I have spent the past twenty-one years working my way through the ranks to land a management position in a Fortune 500 company. I am paid a six-figure salary for my brain, and not my hands, unless you count the time on my computer sending and answering emails. I earn money to lead people in solving problems.

Pan out all the way to see growth. Through careful planning and investments, we have earned and saved enough money for my wife to cut her own path as the owner of A Little Slice of Heaven Bakery* in Decatur, Georgia, which employs five people. We live a life free of creditors, unless you count the occasional credit card debt that we pay off each month.

At times, more than I can count, my country has treated me like crap. Despite this, I love my country and will do anything to defend our way of life and every American citizen. I have faced prejudice, betrayal, and hatred, but I choose to live my life guided by Jesus's words spoken while dying on the cross: "Father, forgive them, for they know not what they do" (Luke 23:34). I learned those words as a young boy in Sunday School. It stuck, and kept me rational when my emotions ran high.

I have worked more than twenty-one years for one of the best employers. But my career has not always been great. From 2009 to 2019, I was rejected twenty-one times for internal job positions. Ironically, I was encouraged by management to apply for some of them. But I continued to improve my brand until I landed one of the best positions in the company.

My life is challenging, interesting, and fascinating to say the least. Where I am today is not where I began. Mentally, physically, emotionally, and financially, my life has come full circle from the

---

* www.alshbakery.com

cross-eyed little boy who grew up in the projects of Greenville, South Carolina to the successful family man living in Metro Atlanta.

As a kid, I saw what life was like around me, and I did what I needed to do to fit in. Trust me when I say I did not always have the best mindset, so I did not always make the best decisions. If you had the opportunity to bet on where my life was headed, you would most likely lose your money.

I can remember hanging out with friends—Charles, Dooney, Shawn, and a handful of others. Shawn and I were the same age while Charles and Dooney were a year or two older. The other boys' ages ranged from nine to fourteen.

We did the things all kids did back then. We walked around and took our chances, finding new ways to have a good time. We would walk to the Boys & Girls Club from time to time, following the train tracks there and back. This was nowhere near where we lived. Thinking back, I'd say it was a good two miles away.

One day, Shawn said, "Hey, I hear they keep a lot of sodas and snacks and stuff inside these caboose cars." We were no strangers to hunger or adventure, so we decided to see for ourselves. We went in one of the caboose cars, and, sure enough, there were sodas and snacks in there. We all took a couple items, and had a ball on the way home.

We got away with it the first time, and maybe got away with it the second time too. The third time we went, we should have known better. That day, Shawn suggested that we visit cabooses at the local train yard. This was different than in the past. We typically raided cabooses located on a single or double track on a single train. Charles and some of the older boys refused and continued the walk home. I followed Shawn. And man, were we two greedy, stupid boys. There were a few trains to choose from, and no one appeared to be around. Therefore, we explored our first caboose and hit the jackpot, or so we thought. As we exited with that day's take, a security guard was waiting for us.

He snatched us up, put us in the back of a car, and threatened to take us to jail. Instead, he took us home so he could tell our parents what happened. I was a kid with no ID and there were no cell phones then, so when he asked me for my home address, I lied because the fear of my mom's wrath far outweighed the time I would have spent in jail.

I directed him to a house I had never seen before, and he left us in the backseat as he prepared to knock on the door. As soon as he knocked the first time we opened the doors, took off running, dashed into the apartment complex, and hid. We thought we had gotten away, but the security guard did not give up that easily. One by one, he asked neighborhood kids if they had seen us or if they knew us. He described us pretty well, and, wouldn't you know it, Shawn's younger brother told him that he knew us! Shawn got in trouble, which meant, eventually, that I got in trouble too.

In some ways, that story is no big deal. I wasn't being malicious. I didn't hurt anyone. That was a normal day in my life at the time. I knew better than to steal from that train, but some days, there wasn't a lot to eat. My mother did the best she could, which sometimes meant grilled cheese sandwiches with the welfare cheese (a rectangular block of American cheese packaged in a box labeled "USDA" that you had to slice yourself) that would not melt. We also had delicious government peanut butter which didn't spread without tearing the bread. Being hungry and seeing an opportunity for food and fun, I decided my moral compass could point in the other direction.

If I continued with that mindset, my life may have turned out very differently. I grew up in poverty, surrounded by marijuana and alcohol. There was bias, desperation, and violence. I had more than my fair share of chances to simply accept things as they were and allow my life to be dictated by my surroundings.

The truth is, I saw and did a lot of things in my childhood that I am not proud of. Eventually, I realized that my circumstances need not be my limitation. One day I made up my mind that while this was my life right now, I would create a completely different future. I would not live in the projects, where friends turned on you just because you were the odd man out that day. I would not be hungry because we ran out of money by the end of the month. I would not wear hand-me-down clothes or be a burden to anyone. There came a moment when I realized my future was up to me, but only if I made vastly different choices in the present.

This book is called *Welfare Cheese to Fine Caviar* because I really did eat welfare cheese, and now I really do have the choice to enjoy fine caviar at an extravagant restaurant—although I have never actually eaten it and probably never will since a few of my friends got sick when consuming the fish roe during one of our annual weeklong vacations abroad. The path in between was not a steady nor a perfect climb. In fact, it has not been a straight line to the top. There have been many turns, pauses, and setbacks. Through focus, patience, determination, and faith, I made it to this point.

I deeply believe that where you start in life does not have to be where you end up. If you *want* to do better and you *decide* to do better, and you go after that with everything that you possibly have, you can make it. Visualize yourself there, and treat everybody well on the way because you can't always recognize the angels that God will send to assist you. Much of my success comes off the shoulders of others. Some of them didn't even know they were helping me. In fact, some had the intent of hurting me. But they had a message for me, and I received it.

State your intentions and go for it. Although everyone and everything is not for you, what is for you will surely come, but only if you hold fast to the vision and remain unwavering in your pursuit. There is no such thing as an overnight success. I did not get out of the projects overnight. I did not finish college overnight. I did not build a career, family, or net worth overnight. Even if it took ten or fifteen years, I decided I was not giving up. I would stick to it and continue to drive until I died. I would either succeed or die trying, as the rapper 50 Cent would say.

Today, I am alive and the challenges are different. Advancing from the poor to the middle class was a huge undertaking. Now my sights are on the upper class, and I am on the path to being totally financially independent.

Even though I've come a long way from welfare, my success story is not yet done. This book is the road map of my life thus far. It is filled with stories that will inspire you, lessons that will help you, and actions you could take on your path. If you're still breathing, if you're still living, then your story isn't done either. Be ready to sharpen your focus, extend your patience, restate your determination, and deepen your faith. You may be able to shorten your journey by learning from my mistakes and delayed actions.

First, change your mind. Then, change your life. And your life will change for the better. Who knows? I may be reading your book, investing in the stock of your corporation, or watching you lead this world to a better future.

This world needs you!

They just don't know it yet.

Poor No More

*When your life is in a ditch,
change your perspective.*

If you listen to young people joking about stereotypes, you might hear stories about how "other people" live. "Other people" do this, and "other people" do that.

More than once, I've heard folks watching and laughing at "other people," making fun of how many people lived under one roof or rode in one car. "So many Mexicans live in that small house," they would laugh. "How do they fit that many people in that broken-down car?" others would ask.

Well, when I was growing up, my family was the same way. We had so many families in the same three-bedroom, one-bathroom, single-level, 830-square-foot house. I remember three uncles, my grandmother, my aunt, my mom, my three brothers (Mike, Lamarcus or Andre and Ronseur), and I living in that house at one time. Multiple people shared beds. We also slept on the floor or the couch.

I was really young then, and didn't care about what we had. In fact, I loved it. My uncles and mom would do skits to entertain the family, and we would be dying laughing. Sometimes Grandma would get involved. Then at 6:00 p.m. and 11:00 p.m., we were glued to the television so that Grandma could watch the news. Even the constant arguments between the siblings were funny. My uncles would fight over one stealing the other's ice cream, but I would not describe it as a fight in today's terms. It was more of a friendly scuffle. Sure, there would be a bloody lip or a few scratches or bruises here and there, but their relationships recovered quickly. *Especially* if any member was threatened or disrespected. I enjoyed having my extended family so close.

It was tough at times, but we made it. When I was seven years old, we finally moved out of my grandmother's house and moved into our own apartment in Woodland-Pearce Homes. After being accepted into a government sponsored housing program, my mom gained her independence from Grandma's oversight. Woodland-Pearce was one of the roughest government-owned housing projects in Greenville, housing about 340 low-income families. We lived there for two years. I was always trying to fit in, but honestly, I just never felt like I belonged.

It was the first of the month and my mom had bought me some brand-new shoes. They were not Nike or Adidas or any other name brand, but they were new. At the bus stop, my friend Percy started picking with me, so we started pushing and shoving each other. Percy was bigger and pushed me and my new shoes into a mud puddle. I was hurt. I went to school with dirty shoes, but that was the least of my concerns.

When I got home, my mom whipped my butt for allowing that to happen. The next day, she went to the bus stop and threatened to beat Percy and his entire family if it happened again. I never experienced problems with Percy again.

My mom had three older sisters and four younger brothers. Growing up, she would have been classified as a tomboy because she spent most of her time with her brothers. She didn't take any mess from anyone.

As time passed, I got used to my new neighborhood. In fact, Percy and I became good friends. I met another really cool dude named Fred. We would play tackle football, basketball, and other sports. We would also explore the surrounding neighborhoods, run store errands for our parents or the elderly for loose change, and perform other odds and ends.

Shortly after starting fourth grade, we moved from Woodland-Pearce Homes over to Crestview Apartments, which was another housing project. Just like before, I tried to get to know all the kids and make friends. I considered myself to be a nice person. I didn't pick fights and tried to get along with everyone, but things were completely different. You had to fight to survive. Every day, it felt like my brothers and I were either fighting or trying to avoid fights. We were either fighting someone in our complex or assisting the boys in our complex fight someone in one of the other neighborhoods.

After about two years, things appeared to settle down. I started hanging out with my new best friend, Charles, and the older kids around. I learned about things like sex, drugs, money, politics, you name it. When I wasn't with the older kids, I spent time playing card games, such as Tonk, for pocket change with my friends Shawn and Detrick.

One day after school, we were chilling out on the stairs. There were probably ten of us—Dooney and his cousins, Detrick, Shawn, and me. We were sitting on the concrete steps perpendicular to Detrick's apartment. Dooney came over to me trying to slapbox. If you've never "slapboxed," it's just what it sounds like. It's boxing, except you use open hands instead of closed fists. I wasn't in the mood to slapbox though, because I knew it would lead to a fight, especially if I was winning.

"Nah man," I told him. "I don't wanna do that."

He wouldn't take no for an answer. On and on he kept pressing me, "Come on, boy." He slapped me a few times on the cheek and pulled me off the step. "Don't be a punk, Thomas. I won't hurt you."

Finally, I was up on my feet, trading slaps. Dooney's cousins watched as Detrick and Shawn continued gambling. Then I did it. I slapped/punched him too hard and bloodied his lip. I apologized, and it seemed that everything was okay. We were friends, right? But one of Dooney's younger cousins kept calling him a punk, saying their family had been disrespected. And just like that, Dooney wanted to fight. For real.

The thing is, I knew that someday we would have to fight because everyone in our complex fights at some point. But I had no interest in fighting my friend. I had known Dooney longer than any other kid in the complex. Unfortunately, I could see things weren't going to turn out well for me. Dooney was there with six cousins; I was there alone. I could only win if I beat all of them. If I did, then I would have to be prepared to do it again and again until someone got seriously hurt. Then the six would grow to twelve and so on. Fights with certain people never ended.

As he and his cousins surrounded me, I did the only smart thing I could do. I jabbed and ran. I ran from our complex to the adjacent neighborhood. They chased me until I got tired, fell in a ditch behind WYFF News Channel 4's building, and balled up to protect my ribs, ears, and face from Dooney and his cousins' punches and kicks.

"Bro, it was an accident!" I yelled. My voice wasn't heard as the punches and kicks continued to pour in.

I could feel my soul exit my body and watch what was happening to me: punch to my head, punch to my arms protecting my rib cage, and a random kick to the side. Dooney and the gang attempted to move my arms. As time stood still, the sequence repeated over and over like a broken record.

What should I do? Stand up and fight like a man? Can I take them all? If I take down Dooney, will I have enough left in the tank to take on his cousins? What if I lose? It was customary for the gang to get a kick in on a kid who had just been knocked out. *If I lie here, everyone will call me a punk.* These were only a small portion of the thoughts and calculations processing in my head.

As I lay there absorbing the impact, I couldn't help but remember how Dooney and I were best friends in fourth grade. I used to help him with his homework. In fact, he was the first to congratulate me after winning the school spelling bees in the fourth and fifth grade, parading me around school as his smartest friend. Something changed when he moved to our apartment complex. He was different. He tried so hard to show people how tough he was. Although I called him my friend, he was more like a bully, at least for Shawn, Detrick, and the other younger kids.

Just the day before, we were all friends (or so I thought). We were all having fun, playing sports, gambling, or fighting other neighborhoods. Everything was good. Then, for no reason, these folks just turned on me. Pounded me like I didn't matter. Like I was nothing to them. No one of consequence.

When the pounding was over, I went back to my house, went into my room, and made a decision. *I can't live like this no more*, I thought to myself. *I can't live in this neighborhood. I can't live with these people. Life has to be better than this.*

I didn't tell my mom about it. Didn't tell anybody about it. But in that moment, I made up my mind to create a new life for myself.

Everything was a struggle. At that time, my mom was on welfare. By the end of the month when the money ran out, it was always a challenge to find something to eat. My father never provided any support to my mom, much less visited me. He was a truck driver and spent his free time riding his motorcycle and picking up women. I later discovered that he had many children spread throughout the southeast. When I was nine years old, he shot and killed his wife as she exited the church after attending Sunday service against his will. He was later captured while disguised as a woman to evade authorities. He died in prison.

Besides Charles and Shawn, I struggled to find real friends. I struggled to find happiness at home. I felt as if I was always in trouble for something my brothers had done. As the oldest, my mom counted on me to be a father figure. So if they were wrong, it was my fault. It was all just too much for me.

When Charles found out about the ditch incident, he found Dooney and beat him. Charles was slightly bigger than me but had an athletic build. In his spare time, he boxed at the local gym. That little accidental bloody lip was nothing compared to what Dooney received from Charles. Dooney was no longer a concern for me. However, his little cousin who started it all continued to be a thorn in my side. I came close to whipping him, but chose to ignore him instead.

However, that moment in the ditch, when my so-called friends treated me that way, was the last straw. At that point, I just decided that enough is enough. *I have to get outta here.* I made up my mind.

I didn't want to sell drugs or do anything illegal, so I buried myself in my studies. In elementary school, I had already been found to be a gifted learner. I had the ability, but up until that point, I hadn't put forth the effort. I got B's with little effort, but I needed A's. It all came naturally, especially math, because I had this inner desire to show teachers that I was not a dumb student from the Hood. When I decided to get out, I knew I would have to be more focused. I would have to live up to my ability. I could no longer do the minimum, if I wanted to be free.

Some people have other talents. They are awe-inspiring athletes or brilliant artists. Everyone has some ability or talent. I was smart, a math whiz. For me, my mind was my ticket out. I was no longer poor because I decided that I was going to achieve the life of my dreams, regardless how long it took.

REFLECTION: *What did you take away from this?*

What was your "in the ditch" moment, when it seemed that your friends or family turned their backs on you? Punches didn't have to be thrown. In fact, the words penetrated deeper. How did it affect you? Was it life-changing?

APPLICATION: *What can you do to reflect on this lesson as it relates to your life?*

Achieving success is the best revenge against your haters. Make up your mind and commit your energy to achieving a better life. You don't have to know all the answers now. In fact, write in a journal what is causing you pain about your current situation. Is it the lack of money, friendship, a future, etc.? Is it something that someone said that hurt, shamed or embarrassed you? Did someone falsely tell you that you weren't going to amount to much in life? Don't hold back. Write it down. This will be what you refer to when you contemplate giving up.

What gifts do you possess? This may be something you're naturally good at, or something you're ready to develop more fully. Write about your gifts in your companion planner. Think about what's going on in your life today. What is it that you're determined to make happen? The timeline doesn't matter, just the intent. Write your own life objective. It is okay to want to be the next famous superstar athlete, singer, actor/actress, etc. However, please understand that you share that dream with millions more which means more competition for fewer opportunities. How hard are you willing to work for it? What is your back-up plan? Consider that there are plenty of stories of superstars who lost their fortune by spending more money than they had, or having it stolen by a slick manager, financial advisor, or family member. Even if you hate it, include mastering math and basic finance as part of your primary plan. Keep and grow what you have worked so hard to earn so that you can reach back and help others.

CAVIAR TIME

Go to the bathroom, bedroom, or any private room that has a mirror. Close and lock the door. Stare at yourself in the mirror. Repeat these words:

"God created me for a reason, and this is not it. My future must be better than where I am now. I commit today to first believe in my abilities to change my life to what I desire. Though I may not be that religious, I believe that God will guide me by speaking to me through my conscience, through the advice received from positive people or by some other means. This can help to expand my knowledge, my network, and my experiences which will seem uncomfortable at times.

I am intelligent. Being smart does not mean that I have all the answers. It means that I realize what I know and that I need to seek answers to what I do not.

I am handsome/beautiful. The name-calling and rejections do not phase me. They are missing out on sharing this great gift that I possess. After I achieve my goals, they will want me more than I want them. If they do not, then there will be hundreds, maybe thousands, of others who will.

God gave me gifts that I will discover and develop. I will achieve my goals or die trying. Every failure will only strengthen my resolve. Thomas Edison failed one thousand times before inventing the light bulb. I have the same or greater potential in me.

Although society seems to hate or ignore me right now, my impact will be huge and beneficial for it. I am somebody with *great* potential!"

PROFESSIONAL TIDBIT

Regardless of their socioeconomic upbringing, some young professionals arrive at a corporation with what I call a "Welfare Cheese Mindset." This mindset consists of one or more of the following:

1. Risk averse – afraid to take calculated risks, even with management approval.

2. Zero accountability – it is always someone or something else's fault.

3. Poor work ethic – late to meetings, doesn't meet deadlines, poor quality of work, and takes shortcuts.

4. Reactive – has limited to no vision, always waits for things to happen versus making things happen, and are physically and emotionally affected by job events.

5. Nearsighted – focuses on the obstacle instead of the overall objective.

6. Self-centered – concerned with what is happening to them instead of what they can do to improve the project or team; only cares about themselves.

7. Misguided – plans to work harder after they receive the promotion instead of making themselves assets that the team cannot do without.

8. Sensitive – receives constructive feedback as an attack on their ability and reputation rather than an opportunity for continuous improvement.

9. Stereotypical – searches for or expects the bad from people versus taking time to get to know people.

10. Insecure – takes their lack of knowledge as a weakness and tries to hide it versus embracing it as an opportunity to learn and better themselves.

11. Inflated ego – focuses solely on making themselves appear great instead of promoting the accomplishments of their peers, manager, or team.

12. Hard-work-only-mentality – believes that their hard work alone will be noticed and result in a raise or promotion. (*Some self-promotion is needed when networking with professionals who can help your career.*)

13. Peer-driven – places higher value on what their friends and coworkers think of them instead of what is best for the corporation.

Don't panic if you possess one or more of these traits. We're human and a product of our upbringing, experiences, and education. The key is to recognize these traits and work to do the opposite. I have done so and have received numerous "Top Performer" or "Exceeds Expectations" ratings throughout my career. In 2010, Bill S., the Vice President of Engineering and Construction, named me one of the ten most influential people in my subsidiary's $3 billion environmental project portfolio. Being a plant engineer at the time, I felt honored to be recognized out of hundreds of employees (maybe more) who worked on the project.

The point is that corporations have invested a lot of time and money in bringing you onboard. They believe that you have potential to be a huge asset for them. They also understand that you do not know everything. They only expect that you hit the ground running by learning the business, contributing in whatever way you can, and getting to know your team and the company. Employees with a "Welfare Cheese Mindset" do not last long.

Stephen Covey's *The Seven Habits of Highly Effective People* is a must-read for any professional who is serious about career advancement. Covey's book will help you in your personal life as well. The seven habits are as follows:

1. **Be proactive.** Respond according to values, be accountable for your actions, understand and increase your circle of influence, and become a transition figure to benefit yourself and others.

2. **Begin with the end in mind.** Create and apply personal and organizational mission statements as constitutions for daily living. Envision the desired results and important values to guide activities and endeavors.

3. **Put first things first.** Focus on what's truly important (i.e., preparation, prevention, values clarification, planning, relationship-building, empowerment). Plan weekly and implement daily based on your mission, roles, goals, and priorities.

4. **Think win-win.** Balance courage and consideration in seeking mutual benefit. Ensure win-win outcomes, despite past win-lose conditioning.

5. **Seek first to understand, then to be understood.** Use empathetic listening, paying attention to another person with compassion, feeling, insight, and emotional identification.

6. **Synergize.** Explore possibilities that will benefit all involved parties.

7. **Sharpen the saw.** Renew your physical, mental, spiritual, and social/emotional lives daily. This will sustain and increase your capacities and help discipline your mind, body, and spirit.

Purchase and read his book today. You won't regret it.

Peer Pressure and Race

An open mind beats a closed fist any day.

When we lived in Woodland-Pearce Homes, I attended Pelham Road Elementary. Pelham was where rich, white people sent their kids. I was neither white nor rich, but I attended this public school anyway. The eighties were the height of Majority to Minority or M-to-M programs. Minorities, usually black kids who were in the majority at their home district, would ride a bus across town to attend better resourced schools. Some kids had to ride pretty far each way. My trip was about five miles.

One of the best things about Pelham was the All-Star Chorus, directed by Ms. Hale. At the time, I had a high-pitched voice and I loved to sing. I auditioned and made the chorus as a tenor. The Pelham All-Star Chorus sang everywhere. We would travel around Greenville and sing at the Shriner's Club, among other nice places. We were very good and were led by a very talented teacher. One day, Ms. Hale told us that we had been selected to sing at the 1984 World's Fair in New Orleans!

I couldn't believe it! However, as exciting as the idea was, right then and there, I knew I would not be able to go. Ms. Hale handed out the permission slips, which listed a fee that I knew we couldn't afford. I reluctantly took it home and convinced my mom to complete the form anyway. When I returned to school the next day, I turned in my permission slip with not so much as a dollar. I wanted Ms. Hale to know I was interested, even though I couldn't pay my way.

Then the unexpected happened. Another parent paid all my expenses for the trip. I was shocked. All this time I had been told, "White people don't want you to succeed," and "You'll always be poor," and all these kinds of negative beliefs. But Pelham Road opened my eyes to other possibilities. Maybe people of diverse backgrounds do want you to succeed. Maybe there is another life beyond poverty.

Someone sponsored my entire trip. They paid for me to go to New Orleans and sing. They paid all my accommodations, and I didn't take it for granted. I attended the trip and gave the best performance my little lungs could provide.

Experiences like that made it easier for me to keep things in perspective, even when people in my environment had other ideas. I was surrounded by people who blamed the government, rich white people, and sometimes even God for their failures. I also noticed that these people had limited dreams. Some had completely given up and would bury their sorrows in a magic eight ball, some other alcoholic beverage, or marijuana.

By the time we moved to Crestview Apartments, I was nine years old. In Crestview, the boys all ran together regardless of age. We'd play sports on our turf, and other times we'd travel to other places and play sports there. Sometimes we would travel to places and fight folks. It was that kind of a crew or gang, as some would call it. Our sport of choice was playing tackle football, without any protection, against the boys in Poe Mill, the neighborhood next to us where the lower middle class of white people lived. In fact, we called it Poor Mill because some of them were worse off than us. Our football games were not for the faint of heart. You ran or caught the ball at your own risk because there were no referees or parents to protect you. You learned to be tough, or smart, and to avoid the occasional clothes-hang, which is when someone reaches their arm out to tackle you by the neck. The bigger boys would run the ball and simply try to run over people, but people like me had to learn how to tackle the big boys at the legs or use my speed and blockers to score.

Crestview, a predominantly black complex on one side of the road, sat right beside a middle-class neighborhood. I can't recall the name now, but I remember the folks who lived there were older and mostly white. Across the street was Poe Mill. You can imagine the three places as a triangle. Black people in the middle, and white people at the other two corners. Some would joke about the black fence around our complex being installed to keep us in.

One day, the Crestview boys were walking to the store, whistling and cracking jokes, having a good old time like we always did. Not far away, we spotted a heavyset white guy and his little brother. They were going to the store as well. The two of them were minding their business, probably not wanting to cause any trouble with our big group of seven boys.

With no provocation, Shawn, one of the guys in our group, started calling the guy "Fatso." Then Charles went on to accuse him of calling us the N-word. My hearing was fine, and I'm positive that didn't happen, but once the accusation was out in the air, the next step was to address it. Who was singled out to handle it? Me.

Status was important to survival, so I had to appear as if I was playing along. If I brushed off my friends, I might've ended up getting my own butt beat. I walked up to the guy ready to swing, but I wasn't into it. I gave him a light push. Nothing serious or dangerous.

Not even enough of a push to send a warning. It was more to save face, to appear I was holding up the code, but his response wasn't as lightweight as mine. He pulled out a knife and lunged at me.

There were a lot of options in that moment, some worse than others. The truth is: that wasn't my fight. I had nothing against him, so I laughed it off. That was a gamble, but it worked. Eventually, he put his knife up. He left me alone and I left him alone, and I headed back to my group. I pleaded my case. "He ain't done anything to us," I told the guys. "Why should we be trying to start a fight when he ain't done anything?"

They called me names. "You a punk, you a punk. Punk, punk, punk. You're a little sucker," and they continued the same story, saying things like, "You let this guy talk about you then pull a knife on you."

I took that and dealt with it. I didn't think it was right to do anything to the guy. He didn't do anything to us. He was walking his little brother to the store, just like we were trying to walk to the store.

It's funny reflecting on the ways decisions come back and visit you again.

Being gifted and in special classes, most of the time I was the only black person there. That, plus the Pelham Road trip, taught me that just because people don't resemble you doesn't mean they're bad people. It's one thing to hear someone claim, "Yeah, we don't like black people, because they're violent, lazy, or they're criminals." But sometimes we put those words in people's mouths. We imagine bad thoughts are floating in other people's minds.

Growing up, I felt that we caused a lot of racial disharmony on our own. We did do stupid things, fought people for no reason and stole sometimes. Then we'd curl our lips at white people. We'd be mad at them when half the time they didn't look in our direction or say a word against us. I wasn't going to fight anybody unless I was trying to defend myself or my brothers.

It was survival of the fittest, but you never knew where you'd end up, like Vacation Bible School and Sunday School at a predominantly white church.

A handful of the kids in the neighborhood attended children's church at Hampton Park Baptist under Paul Hanna. The church provided transportation, and we'd ride the bus. We'd learn about Jesus and God, and how we should be saved. We learned about all the books in the Bible and the different people in it, and we'd get candy, toys, and other treats. I memorized important verses and all the books of the Bible. The stories of Noah, Joseph, David and Goliath, and Jonah in the Old Testament were my favorite. Also, Jesus's statement to His Father that commands us to "Forgive them for they know not what they do" became a motto of mine that I would repeat when faced with adversity (Luke 23:34).

That same kid, the one my friends wanted me to attack, was on the same bus. As it happens, the two of us kicked it off as friends. Imagine what might have been: me beating up a kid because my friends egged me on, and the two of us riding the bus to church every week.

Some might call it a flaw, but I'd like to consider it a strength that I usually trust people first. I give people the benefit of the doubt. I try my best not to stereotype anyone because stereotyping ultimately lands you in trouble. Giving people opportunities and spending time getting to know them, choosing not to react to people's ignorance about my race or my upbringing- this open-minded, and open-hearted approach has opened the doors to new knowledge and ideas. It's brought me exposure to things that have helped me financially, career-wise, and spiritually. This approach has also opened doors for my career, allowing me opportunities to work on challenging projects with German, Japanese, French, and other foreign professionals. These kinds of projects have propelled me and allowed me to have opportunities for promotions and raises faster than my peers.

Having that open mind has been very beneficial.

REFLECTION: *What should you take away from this?*

The few times I based my decisions solely on race, regardless of talent, skill or common sense, were very costly for me. For example, in 2008, a black Atlanta real estate broker who calls himself the "Wealth Builder" stole over $100,000 from us (yes, one hundred big ones). Having paid off our house in November 2007, I was in the market to buy an apartment complex in order to start replacing my income. Purchasing successful foreclosed houses from banks in the past, I used the same real estate agent from the same brokerage to represent me in trying to find an apartment complex to buy. This time, the real estate broker wanted to get involved and provide me a special service. I felt honored.

At the time, I was working on an intense project with a white boss who empowered me, but then would treat me poorly in public. I felt as though I was doing his job but not getting paid or recognized for either of them. Therefore, I was searching for every opportunity to leave my job and start my own business, especially after having earned enough in my commodities trading to pay off our house. When the deal fell through for the apartment complex, because of the broker's recommended mortgage broker not being able to meet his promise of finding financing after vetting us, the real estate broker offered to open a branch of his brokerage in Marietta where I lived.

In this deal, I would invest $100,000 to help open this branch and would split the profits from the agents' commissions with the broker. In fact, he and his wife promised that we would triple our money in two years or less. After reviewing the financial statements of his existing brokerage and visiting his gated house (with his initials on the gate) inside an affluent gated-community, my wife and I were hooked. I attended a few of his investor meetings and was amazed by the crowds. Needless to say, the broker never opened the brokerage. Instead, he stalled me by requiring me to get my real estate agent license and take multiple training classes before getting started, all of which was never mentioned in the beginning.

As I attended countless investor meetings, I noticed that the broker was selling outdated material to crowds that were mostly poor and black. Starting each meeting with how God had brought him a long way and commissioned him to help others, he would hook other God-fearing Christians. After about six to eight months of his stall tactics, I asked for my money back or that he keep his promises. He didn't. After spending over $10,000 in legal fees suing the broker, I won the case, but he filed for bankruptcy. After consultations with my attorney, I decided to walk away versus spending tens of thousands more to try to get what little the broker had. It took every ounce of my being not to take the law into my own hands.

Today, this broker is still at it. In 2018, he had the nerve to send me a LinkedIn request. I responded that I would accept his request if he was repaying me. I never heard from him again. The money was one thing. The years to generate that $100,000 was the main loss. Imagine what business or investment opportunities we missed because of not having that capital.

I was close minded and felt that another black successful person would not take advantage of me. I discredited the seller's agent's warning that my agent did not know what he was doing as it related to the offer for the apartment building. There were warning signs everywhere. And I ignored them all. Do your due diligence on *everyone*. Check past tax returns (at least three years) if you are partnering with someone or purchasing a business. Pay professionals (i.e., lawyers, accountants, etc.) to assist you. Interview clients and competitors and research the market you are entering. The devil can appear in all races, genders, religions, etc.

Are you basing your decisions solely on race, gender, religion, etc.? Are your friends influencing you to do something that you know is not right?

APPLICATION: *What can you do to reflect on this lesson as it relates to your life?*

Are you assigning stereotypes to people because of race, gender, sexual preference, citizenship or other? Are you allowing a bad experience with one or a few people, what you have seen on television, or heard from someone define your perspective of an entire race or group of people? Starting now, smile and greet someone who you normally would ignore. Don't be too sensitive to their responses or gestures because they may be struggling at home or simply not have the same experiences as you. Their response to you may be the product of their upbringing, and how they were treated. For those who use expletive words toward you for no reason, ignore them because they are not worth your time. Search for those diamonds in the rough.

Be wary of organizations or people wanting your money. You have worked extremely hard for that money, and people will come from all over to take it from you. Fight the urge to spend on materialistic items that lose value soon after the purchase (e.g., cars, televisions, and boats). People will say that something will go up in value the longer you hold it. Well, that value means nothing to you unless it is generating income or if there is a buyer willing to pay you more than it cost you. Next, do not give money to everyone who requests it; you cannot help everyone until you first put yourself in a position to do so. Beware of people who use religion to take your money. Tithing and offerings are personal decisions between you and God. God does not want you to be poor. Instead, He wants you to be prosperous, so that you can help bring more followers to Him. Tithing and offering have blessed me in more ways than I can imagine. Most of all, it helps me fight greed. Last but not least, "A fool and his money will soon part" (Proverbs 21:20, King James Bible).

CAVIAR TIME

Go back to your private space used in the previous chapter or find a new one. Close and lock the door. Stare at yourself in the mirror. Repeat these words:

"God has granted me with the knowledge, desire, and characteristics that I need to be successful. The rest is up to me. I can do this.

To achieve my goals, I have to find a diverse group of people to help me. I realize that I must give in order to receive. Without the expectation of compensation, I will give them my attention, my sweat, my respect, and my time in return for knowledge and opportunity. I will smile, even when their words may hurt me, and resist the urge to react with emotion. No person's words have the power to ruin me unless I allow them. I will not always assume that their words are intended to harm me. Instead, I will take stock of the little nuggets of wisdom and education buried in the rough. I will smile and treat everyone with respect. I will greet my elders with sir, ma'am, mister, or missus, unless instructed otherwise.

God will place people in my life to help me and others to test my resolve. I need them both. I got this!"

PROFESSIONAL TIDBIT

The kid who lunged a knife at me is no different than the coworker who tried to attack my character or quality of work, took credit for my work, or lied about me. He perceived me as a threat and chose to attack me to distinguish himself in some way. The mechanic who said that I received my job because I was black is another example. He thought that I would respond with anger or be discouraged. The plant manager who told me I was doing a great job each time I met with him, but told other plant managers that I was not leadership material just before pulling me out of the leadership development program is another. He thought that he ended my upward mobility. I can go on and on. They formed negative opinions of me before I could speak a word, perform a task, or deliver a result.

But I smiled and worked harder and smarter. Before I knew it, I was delivering results on some of the most challenging capital-intensive projects. I had something to prove to myself, not to them. In all these cases, each became a close ally or supporter. As Grandma would say, "Kill them with kindness."

The few times that I responded to those attacks with a little emotion, like frowning or simply ignoring them, I was deemed as the angry black male. This affected my professional advancement. I would receive bonuses and raises but was never considered for management positions because of "something that happened at so and so." The crazy thing is that no one (including me) knew what happened at so and so. This went on for years until Darryl, an angel from above, gave me an opportunity in a new role for the corporation. Having worked with Darryl (when he was a new engineer) in successfully installing, commissioning, operating, and maintaining over $1.5 billion in environmental capital projects over seven years, Darryl knew that I was the only one skilled enough to perform the job. No one else had that experience or exposure. Needless to say, I exceeded everyone's expectations.

Have you ever watched *The Tudors, Versailles, Rome,* or any other medieval movie or television series? Pay close attention to the interactions between the nobles in the court. They attack each other with grace and a smile. A perceived threat to one's honor could lead to death or imprisonment. Therefore, they avoid it unless they want war.

Never respond with anger or too much excitement. If a person upsets you, simply smile, accept the criticism, and walk away. If the attacks persist, discuss the problem with your manager then privately plan how you can turn it into an advantage or simply plan your exit especially if your manager doesn't address it. Outthink your opponents. Always deliver more than expected and treat people like you want to be treated, even if you feel they do not deserve it. No one can take away your performance or your personality. Take the higher ground.

Check out Richard Carlson's *Don't Sweat the Small Stuff*. Richard discusses how often people let little things get them all worked up. Upon closer examination, however, those little things aren't really that big of a deal. He provides nearly one hundred ideas that you can practice to become kinder, wiser, happier, more patient, and less stressed. Other helpful books are Robert Greene's *The 48 Laws of Power* and Sun Tzu's *The Art of War*. Both books are must-reads for the young upward-bound professional. They each use history to discuss the time-tested strategies that people employ to obtain power.

The Thomas Special

Ill intent and revenge lead to a killer headache.

One day I got in trouble with my stepdad for whatever reason, but I didn't think I deserved it. I was only in elementary school, but I often felt my punishments were undeserving; I really had a chip on my shoulder back then. I'm the oldest of four boys, but all of us have different fathers. Mine was the only one who was never around. The last time I saw him, I was three years old.

My stepdad was a few years older than my mom. Before moving in with us, he lived with his parents in Taylors, SC. He had no kids of his own and was employed at South Carolina Steel.

Even though I was a kid, I was pretty much the man of the house. At least that's what I felt. As the oldest boy, I had always been in charge of my brothers. Men would come and go, but whenever they were there, they would take over as man of the house (according to them, at least). If you asked me, it was my domain, and I didn't appreciate anyone coming in to claim my territory. That's where things stood with my stepdad. He pulled rank, and I was in trouble.

He drank alcohol and enjoyed mixing some cocktails. He'd pour them in plastic soda bottles and drink them whenever he was in the mood. That day, I decided to mix a Thomas Special. *I'll show him who's the man in this house*, I thought.

Being the chemical engineer that I ultimately grew up to be, I took whatever I could find—liquors, beers, any liquid I could put my hands on—and mixed it all together. There was nothing poisonous in the batch, but other than that, I was pretty indiscriminate. If you could drink it, I poured it. I adjusted the mixture until it was the same color and consistency of one of his cocktails, poured it in one of those plastic bottles and waited.

Soon enough, he came in and grabbed that bottle. He realized quickly that whatever was in the bottle was not what he had mixed. I was in even more trouble then. As punishment, my stepdad and mother thought I should drink it myself. Not a sip. Not a cup. The entire sixteen-ounce bottle of that concoction. I was a kid, and not a kid who drank alcohol. To make a long story short, I got drunk. Sloppy drunk. I stumbled to my room to lie down. My little brothers tried to tickle my feet and tease me. All I could do was cuss them and tell them to leave me alone.

Eventually, they took me to Grandma's house. I can remember getting out of the car and stumbling over the curb. My grandma tried to comfort me, but I continued cussing everyone.

Grandma fussed at my mom for doing that to me. Now that I know more about alcohol, that was pretty dangerous. Luckily I survived, and all I remember is waking up later at Grandma's house with a killer headache.

You would think that being so young and very drunk, I might not remember this, but it was an unforgettable event. I didn't like the feeling of being out of control. If I thought something, then it came out of my mouth, even if I didn't mean it. I cussed everyone, including my grandma, who did not deserve it. I decided then and there not to drink alcohol ever again.

That situation, observations of my drunk uncle and local winos, and an incident with my uncle a few years later helped me to stay clean. Early on, I vowed I'd never abuse drugs, alcohol, or any substance that could make me lose control of my mind. To this day, I don't drink or smoke. Even in situations where everyone else was drinking or smoking (i.e., basic training at Fort McClellan, college parties, work socials), I'd sit there and watch TV or talk to my friends or coworkers. I've been alcohol-free most of my entire life. I am by no means against adults drinking alcohol casually, but don't get sloppy drunk.

I figured, if I planned to live the life I wanted, I needed to remain focused and on track. The only way to stay focused was to stay in control. So I did.

REFLECTION: *What should you take away from this?*

There are two takeaways from this chapter. The first is that all actions have consequences. You can choose the action, but you can't always control the outcome, especially when you are acting out of revenge. My stepdad didn't deserve me mixing a concoction of his prized drinks. Little did I know, he would become the closest person to a father that I ever had. He would give me money for field trips and take me to regional spelling bees and the other extracurricular events I was involved in. Most of all, he would take me to Grandma's house. He also helped put food on the table at the end of the month when money was low. The punishment that I received was not appropriate, but the lasting result of not abusing drugs or alcohol has benefited me greatly.

The second takeaway is to not allow anything (be it an outside influence like drugs, alcohol or any other type of vice) to control you. If there are things that you want to achieve in life, you must stay focused on the objective because negative influences will cause you to miss opportunities. You could lose sight of the big picture and potentially ruin your life. Most of the people I knew who abused these substances did so as an escape from the stresses that this world placed on them through work, family, school, friends, etc. Alcohol made people cuss and act foolish, while marijuana made them relaxed and mellowed out. As I learned a few years later, the new substances were meant to hook you, forcing you to do *anything* to be able to buy that fix again. They took *complete* control of your mind.

APPLICATION: *What can you do to reflect on this lesson as it relates to your life?*

First and foremost, do not act on revenge. No one ever wins. Instead, let time and God take care of it, whether you are a believer or not. As my grandmother would say, "God doesn't like ugly. Therefore, they will get theirs in due time."

Second, the seed for your future is in your mind right now. That seed is your dreams and ideas. When you focus on them, they start to become your beliefs. Then your beliefs influence your actions, repeated actions (at least twenty-one consecutive days) develop into your habits, and habits define your character. Your character will attract or repel the people who you need to be successful in life. That is why you should remain focused. Your thoughts and beliefs control your destiny. Don't allow people, substances, television, music, or anything else control your mind.

If you watch or listen to anything long enough, then you start to believe that those things are true. Instead, read a book, meet new people, travel to a place that you have never been, listen to a music genre that you have never heard, or visit another church. In other words, keep an open mind that is hungry for new ideas and experiences. Then answer the following:

- What do I want to attain while I am on this planet?
- What education or skills do I need?
- Am I willing to change my character if needed?
- How much effort will I put into this?
- Who can help me?

Share your plans with someone you trust to provide you guidance on your path, but do not share with everyone. Have you heard about the crabs in buckets? Like the crabs, there are some people close to you who will wait until you start exiting the "bucket" to use their claws to pull you back in. Finally, execute your plan with extreme focus and don't ponder on your current circumstances until your objectives have been reached.

CAVIAR TIME

Go back to your private space used in the previous chapter or find a new one. Close and lock the door. Stare at yourself in the mirror. Repeat these words:

"I am intelligent, handsome/beautiful, and loved. I can feel the change that God is making in me. Although I am not experiencing the fruits of my labor, I can picture myself in possession of my goals.

I have met a few people who are helping me. Some don't know that they are doing so. I have met others who are testing my resolve. They continue to mistreat, ignore, or disrespect me. I pay no attention to them and use my anger to push me even harder. I am going to show them. I admit that the first set of insults cut me deep emotionally. However, I have grown thicker skin that is getting harder each day. I will not seek revenge. Instead, I will smile and treat them nicely as I silently recite 'God, forgive them for they know not what they do'. I forgive them. To achieve my objectives, I always need complete focus. One mistake for me could cost me my goals, my freedom, or my life. Therefore, I will not use drugs, drink alcohol, or cede control of my thoughts or actions to any person, group, or organization unless it is helping me meet my objective. Even then, I will question that occurrence to ensure that I am on the right path, especially to consider God speaking to me through my conscience.

In closing, I know this is hard. I see my friends playing and having fun while I study. I do spend some time with them, but I am on a different path. One that will greatly benefit my loved ones and me. I feel the changes stirring in me!"

PROFESSIONAL TIDBIT

Early in my career, I attended a multi-day leadership conference. During the day, we would attend seminars and workshops. In the evenings, we would participate in fun social events that contained a large variety of food and alcohol. This was both entertaining and educational. I would watch some low-level entry supervisors get sloppy drunk and have to be escorted to their rooms.

It was a different story for the executives and rising stars, though. They would drink a little as they worked the room, getting to know everyone. They always remained in control. It turns out that some were working on their next promotion. Sure enough, the announcement would arrive weeks later.

If you work for a company long enough, you will be invited to after-work social events. Never overindulge, because you are always being watched and judged. Some of your peers are measuring their competition while managers are assessing how you would interact with important clients or executives.

Do you know how you should dress for these events? Should you wear a black tie to a black-tie event? (*I did on stage in front of hundreds of small business owners and government officials at a major business conference in Washington DC, sponsored by the U.S. Department of Commerce. Yikes!*) Do you know which silverware you should use for multi-course meals? (*Hint: work from the outside in.*)

Letitia Baldridge's *New Complete Guide to Executive Manners* can help you. From eating with chopsticks to running meetings to entertaining clients, Letitia doesn't miss anything. She will show you how to perform flawlessly in every business situation.

The Death of a Role Model

*Holding a drug addict's money for
safekeeping can be bad for your health.*

When I was fourteen and she was around sixty-four years old, Grandma had a few mishaps that caused the family to worry about her. One day, she became distracted while cooking and burned her arm so badly she had to be rushed to the hospital. She technically didn't live alone, her two youngest sons lived with her. One was a truck driver/mover and stayed out of town during the week. The other worked in construction, partied, and spent nights with his girlfriend(s) at the time. Even though everyone in the family visited Grandma, there was a lot of time that she was alone in the house.

The family wanted someone who would really be there to help her out, to make sure she was okay. I was fine with that person being me. To be honest, I had always been close to Grandma ever since I was a baby. Plus, I wouldn't have to change my high school. Instead of catching the bus, I would walk to school every day. Shortly after starting my first year in high school, I packed my things and moved to her house.

Uncle Rico was her youngest son, and the closest to me in age. He was my role model. He had a car, and any time he'd go places, he'd take me, my brothers, and some of my cousins along. He'd also slip me money for every occasion and would let me do odd jobs to earn a few dollars more. To me, he had it all: money, a car, and women. He'd always have one or two women he was dating at a time. In fact, he hooked me up with the younger cousin of one of his women. That relationship was fun while it lasted.

Double dating with my favorite uncle…priceless. Sucking my teeth, it was easy for me to decide. "Man, I want to grow up to be just like him."

Here I was, living with two of my favorite people: my grandmother and my Uncle Rico, my role models. Those were the times. Life was perfect, or so I thought.

One day, one of my neighborhood friends pulled me to the side at the park and broke some news I didn't believe.

"Hey," he said with a slight grin, "your uncle is on crack."

Crack, short for crack cocaine, was the new drug that completely changed the landscape. Unlike marijuana, crack was so addictive that people would do or sell anything to get the money needed to buy that next high. Mothers would abandon their kids, prostitute themselves, and use welfare checks and food stamps just to have money to buy that next fix. The problem was, the high would last only fifteen minutes or so. Therefore, people spent a fortune in a short period of time and would never achieve the high they did the first time they used the drug. I had been introduced to this drug a few years earlier when I lived in Crestview. The older boys in our crew, including Charles, started selling crack instead of marijuana. They would make more money in a day than they ever could selling marijuana. My friends had new clothes, jewelry, etc. The most I did was hold the drugs; I never used or sold.

I didn't believe my Uncle Rico was a crackhead. It didn't fit with the man I knew. The one with a car, money, and women. The one I saw practically every day. The one I wanted to be like. I blew it off.

"No, you're kidding me," I said. "This ain't true." I shoved him off. In retrospect, this was a dangerous move. "Head," as he was called, was one of the best fighters in the neighborhood and maybe even the city. Shoving him could've been bad for my health. Thankfully, he took it in stride, realizing I was hurt.

I wanted to confront my uncle. On the other hand, my friends had insulted me before. It was a constant game of one-upmanship. Was he pulling my leg to get a reaction? I chose to ignore it and move on. Then one night, a few weeks after my friend dropped the bombshell, Uncle Rico came to me.

I was a good student, and because I didn't get into much trouble Grandma wasn't too strict about bedtime. I'd stay up late, until 11:00 at night or even midnight, watching television shows. When he came, I was up late as usual. Everyone else was asleep.

"Pukey, I want to tell you something." Pukey was the name Mr. Grady, an older man who lived across the street from Grandma, gave me when I was a toddler which has stuck with me to this day.

Uncle Rico sat on the couch, slumped over and grimaced as if he had murdered someone or stole my girlfriend or something. At any rate, it wasn't the same funny, energetic uncle I was accustomed to seeing. He paused, then the words came out of his own mouth. "I'm on crack," he said, crying.

I still didn't want to believe it. "Really?" I asked him. "Quit playing around, Unc."

"Yeah," he said, "I'm on crack." The dejected look on his face combined with real tears, ones I had never seen before, was convincing.

I was fifteen years old and the man of the house for most of my life, so I did what I was used to doing. I put myself in charge.

"All right, I'll tell you what," I said. "We'll tell everybody else, and we'll try to get you some help. Get you in a drug rehab program or whatever. Everything is going to be fine. We can overcome this."

When I told Grandma, she replied, "I knew something was wrong with that boy. He hasn't been himself lately. Plus, he asks for gas money to take me anywhere."

The family was all in. Every family member, including Aunt Barb in Greenwood, lent a hand. We sent him to rehab, gave him moral support, and ensured his son was taken care of. Sadly, it never worked out for very long. He would arrive home clean for a little while, then go hang out with the same crowd that got him hooked and revert to using.

Not only did the family provide support, but his employer, Harper Construction Company, gave him numerous opportunities to get clean. They even held his job while he was in rehab. Uncle Rico meant a lot to everyone. We repeated this for a while until the family was exhausted and gave up. We loved him dearly and never threw it in his face. We also prayed a lot and didn't talk about it, especially in public.

Late one Friday evening, he came in and asked me to hold some money for him. He owed weekly child support for my cousin, his only son. He gave it to me so that he wouldn't squander it. "Don't let me come back and get it," he said. I nodded, determined. I hadn't given up hope in him, or in my ability to help him. *We're going to get through this*, I thought.

I locked both doors to my room so there was no way he could get in and went to sleep. In our one-story, 830-square-foot home, one of my bedroom doors opened to the kitchen and the other to the back porch. This was the earliest I had ever gotten in bed. I woke up when I heard a quiet knock on the door near my room. I heard my uncle's voice calling, "Pukey, Pukey." I heard him, but we had a deal. I lay still and didn't answer the door or say anything at all. Maybe if he thought I was asleep, he would leave me alone.

Soon enough, the knocks moved from the front door to the back porch door to taps on the window. The taps on the window became louder knocks back on the door. The knocks and taps got louder, and now it was kicks and booms. *Boom, boom, boom,* he stomped on the door.

Now he was yelling, "Pukey! Give me my money!" I'm sure everyone in the house and the next-door neighbors could hear, but I stayed put, waiting out the storm. Until suddenly, the stomps turned into one loud "KABOOM!"

He had kicked the door in. When he walked into my room, I couldn't even recognize the uncle I loved so much. His eyes were huge, his face was pale. Zombies were not a big thing back then, but my uncle was the walking dead.

"Where's my money?!" he asked.

My grandma stood right behind him. "Pukey, give him that money right now," she said. And I did. I gave him the money, and he ran off. I didn't see him again for a couple of days.

By the time he returned, he was sad. Disappointed he'd done it again. But I'm not sure he was as sad as I was. He was my favorite uncle, my role model. I admired him. I wanted to be like him. Now, that dream was dead. The uncle I loved was still there, but my role model was gone.

REFLECTION: *What should you take away from this?*

In early chapters, I recommended that you should never allow any person or substance to control your mind, but that is not the lesson for this chapter. The lesson is that you can't save everyone when you are trying to save yourself. In fact, when you fly on a commercial airplane, you hear, "If the cabin pressure should drop, please put on your air mask first, then put on your child's." You can't help your child if you are passed out or dead.

In this case, I felt I could help my uncle get clean by keeping his money secure. However, I could have been seriously hurt if I had stood my ground. Truth is, that was not my uncle standing in front of me. It was his body, but he was being controlled by crack cocaine. The drug called the shots, making him steal from those he loved.

Caution! What I am about to say is not going to sound right. I have had friends in the Hood who were way smarter than me and could have easily gotten doctorate degrees if they wanted. However, they, especially young women, felt that they had to save that drug-addicted parent or sibling. They sacrificed their futures to keep food on the table. Some even dropped out of school so that they could get jobs to do so. In hindsight, I can't help but ask "Was it worth it? Was there another way?" In most cases, there probably wasn't because everyone's family wasn't as close as ours.

I have helped my family many times over after achieving my objective. I have provided cousins their down payments for cars, wired money to relatives in time of need, funded family reunions, multiple celebrations for Grandma, and paid half the funeral costs for my grandma. I could have never done this if I stayed behind to help.

APPLICATION: *What can you do to reflect on this lesson as it relates to your life?*

Is your family dealing with an addiction? If so, is there somewhere you can get help? Is that person willing to accept help? Have you tried at least twice before?

What I have learned numerous times over the years is that you can't help people who don't want help, regardless of what they say. In fact, that person has to take the first step. In my case, it took years (around a decade) for my uncle to control his addiction. It took the family a few years to finally understand that we couldn't save him until he saved himself. We loved and accepted him anytime he came around, but we did not support his habit. He was allowed to live with us from time to time until he stole something (TV, microwave, clothes, etc.), then he was sent to a shelter or somewhere else.

It may sound cruel to treat family like that, but we have too many people in our Hoods that missed out on their dreams because of family. This must end before we force ourselves into slavery or servitude. Don't abandon your dream for anything or any person. Love your family and understand that the best thing you could ever do for them is for YOU to achieve success. Expect pushback from relatives who don't understand your vision. Time will heal those disagreements if they were initially based in love.

CAVIAR TIME

Go to your private space or find a new one. Close and lock the door. Stare at yourself in the mirror. Repeat these words:

"I can feel God working in my life. My attitude and perspective have changed. I accept my surroundings and struggles, because I know that it is temporary. I take pride in every good grade, promotion, or other achievement. I will not let any substance or person steer me away from my destiny.

I love my family and friends dearly. I will teach them what I know, aid them in struggles not self-initiated, and celebrate their achievements. I will not allow their bad decisions to deter me from my goals. This will be one of the most difficult decisions of my life. I understand that I can do more for them once I achieve my goals than I can in my current state. If they love me as much I love them, then they would see it the same way I do.

The path I have chosen is difficult. While my peers seem to enjoy life, I am constantly making difficult decisions and analyzing the results and effects on people. No one seems to understand or believe my vision or why I am constantly out of my comfort zone. However, I dream of me being in possession of my goals. I experience setbacks, but their impact gets weaker each time. I will do this!"

PROFESSIONAL TIDBIT

When I first joined the leadership development program as a young engineer, I met Allen, a young mechanical engineer from Tuskegee University. Allen was a cool brother who would give you the clothes off his back. Although he worked at a plant that was more than twenty miles away, we kept in touch.

Shortly after our corporation was sued for racial discrimination by a handful of former employees, all employees were required to attend diversity training. Allen and I attended one of the first classes. This was one of the most uncomfortable classes. There were twenty or more people in the room and only three black people and even fewer women and other minorities. The subject was about how diversity was a strength, or how they should treat me (or so I thought).

During one exercise, the instructor posted blank sheets around the room. Each sheet covered a demographic (i.e., black, white, gay, women, Baptist, Muslim, Hispanic). Each attendee had to write a misconception that they had heard about each demographic on a Post-it Note, then stick it on the respective sheet. Next, the instructor asked for volunteers to read each sheet.

Allen volunteered to read the one about black people. He had a huge grin as he exited our table, but that quickly changed after he started to read some of the Post-it Notes. Some of the offensive ones included lazy, dumb, and chicken eaters. Tears formed in his eyes.

After reading a few of the notes aloud, Allen turned to his classmates and yelled, "If you all think this about me, then f— all of you." The room went quiet for a few minutes before the instructor cleverly described Allen's frustration as one that all minorities have lived with their entire lives.

I would like to believe that the exercise exacerbated Allen's "Welfare Cheese Mindset," affecting his work relationships and performance. About a year later, my engineering manager requested that I help Allen. He said that Allen was not performing well at his plant. So I did. I talked to him to learn about what was troubling him, shared my experiences and how I overcame them, and offered to help in any way (including helping with his job tasks). He declined my assistance, saying that he had everything under control. A few years later, he was fired for low performance ratings.

I follow Allen on LinkedIn and noticed that he has moved from company to company over the last thirteen years and has not stayed longer than three years at any one company. I attribute some of my later career hurdles to Allen's old plant manager viewing me as Allen.

In Les Brown's *It's Not Over Until You Win*, Les talks about eliminating toxic and energy-draining people from your life in lesson seven. He explains how toxic people are not out to intentionally destroy you; it is simply that the mess they have allowed in their lives will weigh you down. Last, Les states that you can't help or change others until they choose to help or change themselves.

I Am Never Getting Married

True love arrives from an unexpected place.

Although I respected Uncle Rico, Kendall was the one doing everything right. He had the perfect job and helped pay the bills. You name it, he did it. He just did everything right. Well, almost everything.

The one problem was his love life. For years he dated Alicia, a woman who was addicted to crack. They had two little kids, Norris and Harriett.

One Saturday night, I was up late as usual, enjoying an episode of *Saturday Night Live*, when I heard a faint noise. *Tap, tap, tap, tap.* I scanned the living room, wondering what it could be. Was it one of those large rats? Then I heard it again. *Tap, tap, tap, tap.*

I followed the sound to the front door and when I opened it, there stood my little cousin Norris. At that time, he was only about two or three years old. All he wore was a T-shirt and a dirty diaper. I ran out to the street and performed reconnaissance, trying to see who brought him here, but I didn't see his mother or anyone else. *What the heck is going on?* I wondered.

I brought him in, changed his diaper, and got him all cleaned up. Then I woke my uncle up and broke the news.

"Norris just came down here by himself and knocked on our door. I don't see Alicia anywhere," I said. Suffice it to say, he was pissed off.

"That b—" my uncle screamed, ignoring Norris and myself. He jumped out of bed, put on his clothes, and jumped into the car to search for Alicia. An hour or two later, I noticed him pull up to the house. He had found her. They sat in the car for another hour or so until finally Norris and I went to bed.

That was the first time, but not the last time something like that happened. Alicia would use her food stamps and welfare checks to buy crack. Sometimes, she would use money that Kendall provided for the kids. In one instance, she sold the clothes and shoes that Kendall bought for Norris to do so. I'd say it went on a couple of years. No matter what happened, though, my uncle stayed with her. The family tried to convince him to leave and take custody of the kids, but he would never do it.

He loved this woman, through thick and thin. Now, there was one thing that he loved more than Alicia, and slightly less than Grandma: his car. He would spend hours washing, waxing, and detailing that car, and would dare any of us to touch it. One day, Alicia threw a rock at his car and scratched it. I thought she would die that day, but he did nothing. She would tell him that she was cheating and having sex with other men. He'd get upset, but he never left.

One particular day, she had come to our house, and they were arguing about something she had or had not done to Norris. After a while, it wasn't just arguing. They were heading into a full-blown fight. I was only about sixteen at the time, but still I thought that they would argue and go their separate ways, as in previous situations. Then they started physically fighting. For a few minutes, I stood there in shock until, finally, I decided to do something.

Before I could get in between them, Alicia whipped out a razor blade and cut my uncle right across the eye. She barely missed her target. If she had sliced half an inch farther, he would have been permanently blind in one eye.

With his adrenaline reaching its peak, Kendall ran outside, grabbed a big concrete cinder block, and returned to the house. Instead of fleeing, Alicia stood there daring Kendall to respond. *What is she thinking?* Before I could finish the thought, Kendall swung for her head.

I got in between them the best I could and tried to keep them apart. I didn't like the fact that Alicia cut my uncle, but I was not about to let him make a mistake that would ruin the rest of their lives and that of my little cousins.

There I was, still in the middle and blood dripping down me, doing all I could to keep a bad scene from getting even worse. Finally, Grandma's words, with me in between the two, broke them apart. Alicia sprinted out of the house. Uncle Kendall was still heated and said all kinds of vile things. "I can't believe that b— cut me. I am going to kill her ass."

"That's not the right thing to do. You're bigger than that," I told him. "Let's just get in the car and go to the hospital emergency room."

"What about Norris?"

"Grandma got him," I replied.

Eventually he calmed down enough to get into the car. He drove and I sat in the front seat. I helped him navigate while blood dripped down the right side of his face.

I remained by his side while he got stitched up, then we headed back home.

Could I have anticipated this and acted sooner, preventing my uncle from getting cut or Alicia from receiving that small lump on her head? Prior to then, I had never seen a man and woman in my family fight like that. I was expecting them to yell, argue, talk for hours (maybe taking a day for that argument), and then kiss and make up.

When they started fighting and that blade came out, I could have stood on the sidelines, crying or watching. I could've ignored the whole thing. I could have responded with anger and jumped in, trying to defend my uncle or something like that. However, none of those options were the right thing to do. There could be no winner in that situation. Either one could've ended up seriously injured or dead. Besides that, these two adults were parents. My cousins' parents were fighting each other like mortal enemies. It just didn't seem right. I didn't care how bad of a mother Alicia might have seemed at the time it just wasn't right.

One lasting impression this had was not to align myself with anybody who would make me upset enough to want to fight. I was not going to hit a woman. Being privy to that kind of situation can end in one of two ways: you can continue that cycle in your relationships or you can create your own pattern. I was determined to create my own.

In high school, when I started dating, I did my best to treat the girls with love and respect. I wanted to cultivate positive interactions with women, so I checked for traits. I was very careful about how they responded to me and how I responded to them. Did we create violence together or love?

Tina was my first love. We dated throughout high school until my freshman year in college. I was the only guy she wanted, and I was faithful as well…until peer pressure and hormones kicked in. One day, I accompanied my best friend James to meet his girlfriend and her cousin, a girl who I initially started talking on the phone with only to help James, but then had grown to like. We met the girls in front of the movie theater. As they exited the theater, James took his girlfriend to the front of the car by the hood, and I had her cousin at the back. We were laughing and having a good time out in the open.

"Thomas, is that you? Thomas!" It was Tina and her older brother, Darrell. My heart dropped as I saw the tears of sadness, disappointment, and anger drip down her face. Her brother shook his head in shame.

James, being my best friend, said, "T, let's go." I got in the car and didn't talk to Tina for a few days. She would call, but I would not answer because I was ashamed. I had sacrificed the love of my life for someone I did not want to be with long-term.

Eventually, I came to my senses, apologized, and got Tina back. Our relationship was better than ever. The love that Tina displayed was true love. She always greeted me with a huge smile, a passionate hug, and an affectionate kiss. Most of all, she was extremely loyal and never let any other boy get past "Hello." She had her dream man and didn't want anyone else.

Deep down, I didn't think marriage was for me. I'd seen a lot of infidelity, violence, and money issues. I just didn't experience many examples of healthy, happy, and loving relationships. Ultimately, I felt I'd never make that kind of commitment.

After her mom died, Tina decided to forego college so that she could take care of her dad. Her older brother was already studying electrical engineering at the University of South Carolina. This was admirable and displayed the deep affection Tina provided the people she loved.

During my freshman year, also at the University of South Carolina, we tried to make the long-distance relationship work. Since I didn't have a car, Tina would drive almost two hours to see me on the weekend. There were just two problems. There were too many women showing interest, which I handled easily by telling them that I had a girlfriend I loved. The second was our goals changed. We had talked about college, marriage, and kids many times during our relationship. But her goals had shifted. She couldn't see anything past staying at home to help her father. For me, my only goal was to achieve my degree and have a better life. We grew apart until I made one of the hardest decisions in my life at that time, and I broke up with her.

Every girl after Tina was just someone to have fun with, some not lasting more than one night. No one could ever love and be as devoted to me like Tina. In fact, I never gave them a chance. If we started a relationship and I sensed something was wrong, then I quickly ended it. Tauria, a girl from Bermuda, was the longest relationship that showed promise, until she wrecked my car. I ended our relationship shortly thereafter.

I was never going to be married. The problem was not the girls I was meeting. It was me. My vision of the ideal woman was completely screwed up. Plus, that woman could not interfere with my goals.

Then I met someone.

Melanie was an engineering major like me, so we ended up in a Statics class together, an entry-level mechanical engineering course that studied the forces affecting stationary objects. She was beautiful *and* intelligent. The problem was that she knew it, which was a huge turnoff for me. We were friendly, and I didn't see much beyond that, but I did want her to succeed. Being the whiz that I was, I tutored her, but that was it. We remained friends, dated other people, and went on with our lives for a year or so.

One summer, after I'd broken up with Tauria, I bumped into Melanie on campus. She was returning from a Co-Op and I was returning from a semester at North Carolina State University as part of the National Student Exchange Program. We said "hello" and caught up on each other's lives. We were good friends. She was talking to a couple of guys at the time, but nothing serious. For a few weeks straight, we spent every day together. We would go to the movies, the bowling center, Putt Putt (miniature golf), or just walk in the park. We would discuss long-term goals and visions of the ideal family life. That was enough to light the spark, and we began dating shortly after that.

Even though we were quite close, I was hesitant to propose. After everything I'd seen, I still didn't want to make the wrong decision. We did eventually settle down and get married, but it took four years. I was cautious, mindful of what I knew, yet focused on what I wanted to create instead. Our wedding was one of the happiest moments of my life.

REFLECTION: *What should you take away from this?*

Behind every successful person is an even stronger spouse. Melanie, my wife of more than nineteen years, as of 2020, is beautiful and intelligent. Most of all, her goals align with mine. Together, we have built a successful family with two handsome boys to show for it.

I experienced several women before finding Melanie, and each had good qualities. I identified qualities that I wanted in a woman. If a woman rejected me, then I simply moved on. If we started dating and I noticed that she smoked or drank alcohol excessively, then I ended the relationship. If I observed her cheating or flirting with someone else, I cut her off. If she did anything that signaled that she was about to prevent me from achieving my goals, then she was history.

It sounds cruel. I loved some of those women, and it was hard to walk away. But I had to change my way of thinking. I was already committed to achieving my dreams of escaping poverty. It was just as much of an honor for the girl to be with me as it was for me to be with her. I had tremendous potential that was going to benefit both of us. Besides, how long would she stay with me if I struggled financially?

APPLICATION: *What can you do to reflect on this lesson as it relates to your life?*

Be careful who you choose to date. Be even more careful with whom you decide to have sex with. Even if you avoid catching sexually transmitted diseases, one mistake could tie you to that person for the rest of your life, or at least eighteen years of it. In other words, do not have unprotected sex or sex of any kind with someone you don't want to spend the rest of your life with. Don't commit to anyone who has an addiction to drugs or alcohol. Your love will not help them. Instead, their addiction could drag you into its trap. Don't commit to someone who has issues with a family member who you love dearly and trust. For me, it was Grandma. If Grandma didn't like her, then she was not for me.

When you date someone, decide what qualities you want in a spouse. Then be patient, have fun, and wait. Slowly discuss long-term goals and objectives, being careful not to overload that person. It is probably best to discuss at least one goal a week or as many as your mate is willing. How does your mate respond? Do they tell you what you want to hear? Is it genuine? Do they tell you the truth even if it hurts? The truth is what you want. Do their actions match their words?

Don't fall obsessively in love with the first person who loves you. It is rare that you will remain with that person forever. Give it your all, but don't do anything stupid out of love because that person wronged you or decided to break up with you. Rejection will come from time to time. With every rejection comes someone who is even better. If ninety-nine percent of the men/women in this country don't like you, there are still one million women/men who do. If you travel internationally, this number is even greater. As Grandma would say, "Pukey, there are plenty of good fish in the sea. You just have to be extremely careful where you stick your fishing pole."

Long-term relationships are full of compromises and adjustments. However, don't let anyone or anything prevent you from achieving your goals. There are so many traps you must avoid. If you must choose between a mate and your dreams, always choose your dreams. If someone truly loves you, they will never come between you and your objectives. Remember for a relationship to work, both parties must want it to succeed and work hard each day at it. If one party doesn't, then it is best to walk away.

CAVIAR TIME

Go to your private space or find a new one. Close and lock the door. Stare at yourself in the mirror. Repeat these words:

"I am blessed and highly favored. I can see my life-changing for the better. I have met some great people who have helped me, and others who have strengthened my resolve. I acknowledge that I still have a ways to go.

I have dated some beautiful people, only to discover that beauty is sometimes skin-deep. When one of them wrongs me, it hurts. I press on because my future is more important than any one person. I trust that God will bring the right person into my life. Until then, I will enjoy meeting new people and having fun.

This path continues to be difficult at times. Most people close to me do not see the world, much less the future, the way I do. I still love them. In fact, it hurts when I have to distance myself from them or cut them completely off to secure my destiny.

My dreams of me in possession of my goals are becoming clearer. I can see the path that I need to take. I experience setbacks, but their impact gets weaker each time. Most of the time, they reveal unforeseen paths to success. God is on my side!"

PROFESSIONAL TIDBIT

Do you think you can keep your personal life separate from your professional life? Think again. You spend most of your awake hours at work, approximately 45 percent of a seven-day week. This number approaches 50 percent, depending on your commute and the amount of business travel. That is a long time to hide emotions that may have originated at home. Just ask Ryan.

Ryan graduated from Georgia Tech with a mechanical engineering degree. Not only was he extremely smart, but he was also personable and empathetic. Everyone—managers, secretaries, and janitors included—liked Ryan. He was a rising star.

At that time, Ryan was dating his college sweetheart, who had to have been a cheerleader. By the time she became his fiancée, she'd become an attorney at a big law firm and was already starting to make a name for herself. Their wedding was extravagant, not a detail missed. They both seemed so happy. Then they purchased a new home and cars.

Ryan had everything going well for him: a beautiful wife with a promising career, an upward path to executive management, and an expensive home in a premier school district. Everyone, including me, wanted to be like Ryan: living a Ken-and-Barbie, Beverly Hills lifestyle, without having to work twice as hard for it. (But there are some things I can't change about myself.)

After the couple had their first child, things changed. Ryan's wife quit her job to stay home and raise the baby. Being old-fashioned, Ryan supported that move. Over the next year, Ryan's demeanor began to change. Normally at ease in all situations, including crises, Ryan reacted negatively to everything.

Caring about my friend, I invited him to lunch. Ryan was under a lot of financial stress. In addition to the mortgage and auto loans, he financed a large fraction of the wedding costs including the honeymoon using his credit cards. It turns out that Ryan wasn't the rich white kid I had envisioned.

"Chill," I said empathetically. "The best way to get out of this hole is to stop digging."

"But my wife has expensive tastes," he replied helplessly.

"Well, you have to make a choice," I said as if I were his father. "If you continue on your current path, you will not have a job because no one will want to work with you."

I pulled out a napkin and had the waitress bring me a pen. I did what all chemical engineers do when performing material and energy balances. I drew a box. First, we constructed the arrows leaving the box (i.e., loan payments, cost of living expenses like utilities, car maintenance, taxes, and other cash outflows). Second, I listed what was in the box like savings, checking, investments accounts, cash under the mattress, etc. Third, we drew the arrows entering the box. For him, the only cash inflow was his salary each month. Finally, I asked him to take the napkin home and fill in the blanks. Using a simple formula (total inflows subtract total outflows), I asked "Is the box shrinking?" In other words, are you spending more than you're earning? I didn't want to know his salary, because it would probably have upset me.

The next day, he arrived at work a new man. His box was shrinking but was recoverable with a few lifestyle changes. Now the hard work began: convincing his wife. They took my advice and met with a financial planner. Over the next few weeks, they had some tough discussions, but their love conquered all in the end.

My pastor, Bishop Dale C Bronner, once said, "Women enter marriages thinking they can change their husbands, while men enter marriages expecting that their wives will not change." Both are flawed expectations. Before you decide to get married, check out Marlo Thomas's and Phil Donahue's *What Makes a Marriage Last* and Gary Chapman's *The 5 Love Languages: The Secret to Love That Lasts*. You can have a long, successful marriage if both of you are aligned and commit to working on the marriage throughout.

Control Your Response

Inaction is often the best reaction to crazies, especially those in authority.

Most freshmen start college in the fall semester. I didn't start until the spring. Instead of going to school, I joined the United States Army Reserve as a Chemical Operations Specialist (Nuclear, Biological, and Chemical), and headed to training at Fort McClellan in Anniston, Alabama. My recruiter said it would give me a head start on chemical engineering, my chosen field of study in college.

Coming out of high school, I was offered a full tuition scholarship from Fluor (Daniel) Corporation and a smaller one from Delta Sigma Theta Sorority. I was blessed to have the money to be able to attend school and perform my studies, but I just didn't feel ready. I felt that I wasn't disciplined enough and even though I had the tuition, there would be other costs I couldn't afford without loans.

Therefore, I decided to meet with military recruiters. I had two cousins and an uncle who had served in the United States Marines, Navy, and Army. I remembered when they first went into the military, and I remembered the difference in them when they came out. They became very disciplined people. Role models. I figured it would have the same effect on me. I prayed over it a lot, and eventually I decided that it was the right thing to do.

I didn't want to have a full-time career in the military. I wanted to graduate with a chemical engineering degree and hold a civilian job. So the US Army recruiter offered me a $10,000 student loan repayment and a MOS (job) that he said was similar to my major. There was also a General Issue (GI) Bill that would provide a monthly allowance. All I had to do was spend one weekend a month, and two weeks every summer, with the military. Additionally, the locations for the drills were convenient to school and home.

After I signed up, I went home and didn't tell anyone the news until a couple of weeks before having to report. I even forgot to tell Fluor and Delta Sigma Theta. Therefore, I lost both scholarships, but was able to recover the Delta Sigma Theta one later. In fact, my mom still has my Fluor certificate identifying me as a scholarship recipient. Nonetheless, the adventure began.

When you first get processed in, they do a little bit of yelling at you, but it's not that bad. It's nothing most kids haven't experienced at some point or another. It's like a football coach yelling on the sidelines. Sometimes they get a little heated, but it's no big deal. For the most part, everyone was in a decent mood. Some tried to show how tough they were, but turned out to be the first to crack. Others couldn't handle it and were soon sent home. The rest, like Love, Diggs, Alvarez, and I, were laid back, but observant. Although we didn't say much, there was quite a bit of communicating with our eyes and facial expressions.

We got our IDs made and quickly learned the motto that would stick with us the remainder of the camp, *Hurry up and wait.* We would wake up early, exercise, and then sit for an hour. We would then rush to Supply Chain to get our uniforms, duffle bag, and other supplies and wait for what seemed like hours to get everything we needed and processed. During the down periods, we were completely bored because we had no access to books or electronic devices. We were completely shut out from the outside world. This went on for a little over a week until we were finally assigned to a battalion and company.

Then, D-Day, the day we reported to our battalion and were assigned a drilling instructor who would be with us the remainder of the training, arrived. It wasn't as bad as D-Day of 1944, the invasion of Normandy. We boarded buses and headed to our new barracks with duffle bags so full that we had to carry them with both hands and straps around our shoulders. The bags were heavy, loaded down with all our equipment and everything else we needed. As we sat on the bus with duffle bags in our laps, we could barely move and see in front of us. As the bus crept along, there was a sense of happiness, fear, and anxiety. For me, I was ready to start, and complete, training so that I could start college.

After a few minutes, we pulled up to the barracks. I was excited, thinking, M*an, I can finally get rid of this duffle bag*. Then the drill sergeant appeared. He boarded our bus and kindly greeted everyone. Then a light switch flipped in his brain as he proceeded to scare the holy daylights out of everybody. He started off with "Y'all, maggots," and it went downhill from there with screaming and cussing at all of us.

"Get your asses off this bus and into formation now, Privates!"

It was intense. No more innocent excitement or fond memories of football coaches. This was serious business.

As we exited the buses, we noticed drill sergeants yelling and screaming everywhere. We rushed to formation with those duffle bags that suddenly appeared to be lighter. Once we got in formation, they made us do push-ups because we didn't move fast enough. Then, we would get back in formation and had to do push-ups again. This went on for probably an hour. During this time, drill sergeants were singling out people and making them do more pushups as they yelled and cussed in their ears. Then, we got back in formation and had to hold our military ID so they could read it. Not just anywhere, mind you. You had to hold it right at your ear. And wait.

There you stood, holding your ID perpendicular to your ear, neither moving nor speaking unless spoken to. Just waiting. I stood there for thirty minutes before it was my turn to tell my name and social security number. Standing there holding that ID in exactly the right spot is as tough as you think it is. Every time you were caught adjusting or shifting your arm, the drill sergeants got in your face and made you do push-ups.

One of them, Drill Sergeant Collins, came over and peered in my face. "You are from the Hood, aren't you? Come with me." I followed him, and he led me up to the top floor of the barracks.

"It's just me and you right now. Just me and you. I can see it on your face. You want to fight me. If you want to fight, you can do whatever. It's just me and you. I'm going to take this hat off. We can go at it right now."

What do you say to that? Nothing. The answer is you don't say anything. You don't do anything. He goaded me, trying to provoke a response.

Finally I said, "No, sir. I don't want to fight. I did everything you told me to do."

"Private, I ain't no captain! I work for a living!" he screamed.

He was relentless. There were maybe three to six inches between his nose and mine, if that. He was literally in my face, and when he talked, spit flew from his lips. I was fresh out of high school and this grown man was huge, much bigger than I was. I was scared, afraid he might try to push me or instigate something and get me thrown out.

"No, Drill Sergeant. I do not want to fight."

Again and again he'd try to provoke me, but I did not take the bait. In the back of my mind, and, at this point it was in the very far back, I knew I was there for a reason. I was there to graduate from basic training and advanced individual training (AIT). I was there to get disciplined, and to get help to pay for college. That was my goal.

Could this have been avoided if I smiled or something? Growing up, you didn't walk around smiling unless you were with your boys, or with family, because someone might decide to test your courage. Therefore, it was best to glower at others like two heavyweight boxers after shaking hands, especially if you were visiting a different neighborhood. You also couldn't overdo it because people could easily pick up that you were putting on a front. The key was confidence. The best fighters, like Charles, never advertised their talents, but I saw many boys dropped by their hands.

That drill sergeant did all he could to shake me from my path. I couldn't let that happen. I couldn't lose focus. I stood there and took what he dished out. Eventually, he led me back out and put me back in formation. By then, they'd moved on to the next recruit.

It was just a crazy experience; the military broke me down to my near breaking point and stripped away all my pride. Then they built me back up and made me more disciplined, more patriotic, and more mentally and physically fit. In fact, I was prepared to overcome any enemy, physical or abstract, or die trying.

Drill Sergeant Collins, the one who administered that first test, was probably one of the most admired drill sergeants we had. I thought the world of him. Why? Because he put even greater effort into building me into a strong soldier and man than he did breaking me down. The yelling and screaming turned into encouragement, respect, and compliments when he noticed I was giving all that I had.

That experience plays into the whole puzzle of my life. To be honest, I was scared. Scared of failing. I wanted to make sure I did everything I possibly could to achieve my goal. I needed discipline, and I needed financial support, so I went and got it.

REFLECTION: *What should you take away from this?*

If I feel that I need something to achieve a goal, I am not too shy to go after it, regardless of what it means. If that means I must fly over to Siberia and spend two weeks in the desert to achieve a goal, I will do it because that's what it takes.

That's how strong that goal was to me at the time. I did not want to be poor. Everything goes back to not wanting to be poor. To wanting freedom and the ability to go where I want to go, buy what I want to buy, and do what I want to do.

One telltale sign that you are headed in the right direction is the adversity that you face. Life throws obstacles in your way to see how bad you really want it. As my grandmother would say, "The devil will always test you when you are doing something good." I wanted to give up early in basic training. The constant screaming from the drill sergeants, lack of sleep (only four to six hours per night), and physical exertion from physical training (PT) was demanding. I was both mentally and physically exhausted, but I stuck with it and did not allow it to break me. Each day got a little better, until after twenty-one days when it became a normal routine. After graduating from military training, I could conquer anything.

APPLICATION: *What can you do to reflect on this lesson as it relates to your life?*

What will you do when faced with challenges? Is your goal important enough for you to skip a meal per day so that you can save for a needed textbook or class, to not retaliate to a slap or spit and to walk away when you know you can physically beat your opponent, to be rejected numerous times before getting a chance, to be insulted about the clothes you wear, to be harassed or wrongfully accused by local authorities? The world expects you to respond a certain way and will send test after test. Remember, success in achieving your goals is the greatest revenge.

In a prior chapter, you chose a goal(s) that you want to achieve and decided on how much effort you are willing to put forth toward it. Jot down how you will respond when faced with challenges. Prepare yourself mentally. What will be the first thing you do when you reach your goal? How will you celebrate your sacrifices?

CAVIAR TIME

Go to your private space or find a new one. Close and lock the door. Stare at yourself in the mirror. Repeat these words:

"God continues to throw difficult tests at me. At times, I want to quit and take the easier path. But I know that He doesn't test me on anything that He has not already prepared me for. The more I overcome, the stronger I get.

I have experienced times when it has been extremely difficult to not respond by punching, slapping, or hurling cuss words at someone. I know that I would not be fighting them alone. Society does not see my vision and potential, nor cares. Instead, society is waiting in the background for me to slip, so that I can be placed in jail if I am lucky. I am not the person they see in their stereotype. God, please forgive them for they know not what they do.

God is shaping me into someone who will have a positive impact on society. I will help improve the lives of ALL, regardless of their perception of me. The more people I help, the greater the blessings that God gives me. No one will stand between success and me!"

PROFESSIONAL TIDBIT

Chiquita was a talented electrical engineer from the University of Florida. But, man, was she overly sensitive. Any little thing could set her off.

One morning, our manager didn't respond to Chiquita's greeting. She repeated herself louder, almost yelling, then the manager responded.

"I think he is prejudiced," she said after the manager walked away.

"No, he is just a butthole to everyone—white, black, family, etc." I responded, referring to past observations of him in meetings and at annual family picnics at the plant.

"I hear you, but I think the man has a problem with black people, especially black women," she snarled.

The manager treated everyone that way. There were numerous times that I would greet him with "Good morning, Rich" only to receive no response, sometimes not even a smile. But that didn't bother me. In fact, Rich was a very intelligent and resourceful engineer who rewarded his people handsomely for delivering positive results. He just had terrible interpersonal skills.

At the end of the year, Rich met with us individually to discuss our performance. I received a rating of "Above Expectations" and Chiquita received "Meets Expectations." She was livid. She went to her cubicle for thirty minutes then visited mine and grabbed me by the arm, taking me to a private room so that we could talk.

"He had the nerve to say that I needed to improve the quality of my work, arrive to meetings on time, and not spend so much on meals during business travel!" she screamed.

"Calm down, Chiquita," I replied. "On the surface it sounds bad, but you received a 'Meets.' You can bounce back from this."

"I'm going to report him to Ethics," she said as if a light bulb had turned on in her head.

"Be careful," I cautioned her. "On what cause?"

She didn't respond. Later, she came to her senses and decided not to file a complaint. She never fully recovered, however. A few months later, she left the company and moved back home to Florida.

Chiquita could have easily become a manager in our company once she cleaned up a few bad habits. In fact, our manager mentioned that during her performance review. She was one of a few women engineers in the company. At that time, there was a push to coach, train, and mentor women engineers into leadership roles.

In Napoleon Hill's *Think and Grow Rich*, Napoleon talks about how you cannot achieve anything if you do not take control of your thoughts and actions. He states that we are creatures of habit, but, because we are a mind with a body, we can change our habits. "If you do not conquer self, you will be conquered by self" is one of my favorite quotes in the book.

Think first and act afterwards. Shape the patterns of your thoughts to harmonize with your goals and purposes. Keep your mind busy with a definite purpose backed by a definite plan of action. And you will soon discover that unexpected events, including crises, do not affect you as much as they affect everyone else.

The Payoff

The pathway to earning more while working less lies in your head.

I made it. I finally made it. Graduating college and getting my first job offer was one of my happiest moments. I had worked so hard to go from having nothing to finally having something.

Early in my senior year, I began reaching out to companies for jobs after graduation. I sent out my résumé and did a number of interviews. Some of them didn't turn out quite the way I expected. One experience was particularly memorable.

As an engineering student, I attended the National Society of Black Engineers (NSBE) Conference in Anaheim, California, free of charge thanks to Eastman Chemical Company. At the career fair, I met a manager from General Mills. After giving her my elevator pitch, she smiled and encouraged me by saying, "Come interview with us. You've got to come interview with us."

What is an elevator pitch? If you and someone who's in the position to help you are on an elevator, what would you say to gain their support in the thirty to sixty seconds it takes the elevator to reach your floor?

It was music to my ears. She seemed so enthusiastic. Her energy excited me, and I was sure that's where I'd end up working. Over the next two weeks, I received a call to discuss travel arrangements. They took care of almost everything. The flight, hotel, and all other accommodations. A week later, I traveled to Minneapolis, Minnesota, ready to rock the interview and get the job.

Well, I arrived at the baggage claim and scanned for my name on the signs held by chauffeurs, or anyone showing an interest to pick me up from the airport. I soon discovered I was there on my own. No one had made arrangements for ground transportation. There was no such thing as Uber or Lyft yet, so I had to figure it out by myself.

I was starting to feel a little unsure about things, but I was determined to get that job. I was too close to being deterred by what I assumed was a mistake. I caught and paid for a cab to the headquarters. However, when it was time for my interview, I never even met the manager I thought I was scheduled to see. I ended up meeting with several other people individually in their offices, and all but one of the interviews went well. During one interview, I was asked a series of technical questions for which I had not prepared. It was disappointing, but not surprising, that I didn't get an offer. I was, however, reimbursed for all expenses.

Later, I found out my friend and classmate had a completely different experience with them. Someone picked her up from the airport, and she ended up with an offer in hand. Also, she only had one interview and it wasn't technical. That experience stands out in my memory, but I had several other interviews that semester including one with Merck, the pharmaceutical company.

As my senior year came to a close, I wasn't sure where I'd end up. The truth is, I was a little stressed out. As I got closer to graduation, I kept having nightmares that I didn't turn in something, or I didn't complete an exam, or something had gone wrong. I felt like everything I lived through was just a fairytale, and I hadn't done anything.

This wasn't true, of course, but I couldn't shake the feeling. More than anything I wanted to make something of myself. To make good on that determination from my childhood.

I was closer than I gave myself credit for. For one thing, I was a Carolina Eastman Chemical Company Scholar. In my sophomore year, they awarded me a full-tuition scholarship. I had been working summer internships with them, and, during Christmas, they let me come and work with them to make a little money. They expected a return on their investment in me, and the vice president heavily recruited me to come work for them. On top of that, they paid all the expenses for my classmate and me to attend the NSBE Conference in Anaheim mentioned above. At the end of the year, they offered me everything I could want. Financially speaking, they had the best package. Given my goals, it seemed obvious that I should work there.

But I had my own ideas. I just didn't feel comfortable going to work at the company. I was forward-looking, or so I thought. They made plastic pellets and I believed that industry was cyclical. I thought if I were to go and work for them there, I might be out of a job in a few years. And although they were close (Columbia, South Carolina), the truth is, I wanted to be around my family in Greenville. So there I was with an offer I wanted but didn't get, and an offer I should've wanted, but wouldn't take.

Then, one day, Bert Nagy called. It's been over twenty years, but I still remember his name. Bert was the Process Engineering hiring manager at Fluor Corporation. Fluor is an engineering and construction corporation headquartered in Irving, Texas, but they had an office in Greenville they received when they acquired Daniel Construction.

I'd done well in my interview, so Bert called and praised my performance and credentials, and he just couldn't say enough great things. He told me everything I wanted to hear, then he said the magic words, "Hey, you've got a job offer, if you want it."

By the time that call ended, I was ready to go work for him. I didn't know how much I'd be making or any of the details; I just knew Fluor was the right place for me. Bert told me to expect the email offer soon and to let them know within the next week if I would accept it.

I checked my email from the computer lab at school. Sure enough, the offer came in. I saw the numbers and my eyes popped open and a huge smile spread across my face. The industry, money, and location were all exactly what I wanted. I vibrated with joy, happy at the thought that I'd finally made it. I floated to class on cloud nine.

Let's pause and discuss the offer. Prior to college, I made about $3.00 - $4.00 per hour as a dishwasher at local seafood restaurants. I bust my butt for each hour washing dishes, shucking oysters, assisting the cook, and cleaning up at the end. During the summer after completing my first semester in college, I got a job at an AutoZone warehouse, earning about $6.00 per hour by fulfilling orders for automobile parts. It was a step up, but not worth the daily back pain and the fact that I dropped a brake rotor on my unprotected big toe as steel-toed shoes weren't required at that time.

In college, I entered the cooperative education program (Co-Op) during the spring semester prior to starting my sophomore year and received $9.75 per hour to sit on my butt and solve problems using my brain. The following summers, my wage rose to $13.00, then to $16.00, and $18.00 before earning my degree. The Fluor offer was going to pay me almost $25.00 per hour ($50,000 per year), benefits, and two weeks' vacation to not break a sweat, hurt my toe, or go home wet and smelling like fish. It was a no brainer. That was a lot of money in December 1998. In 2020, the average starting salary for a chemical engineer was closer to $75,000 (about $36 per hour).

As a child, I made the decision early that I was not going to be poor again. I had pretty much razor-sharp focus on trying to succeed. It just felt like everything that I worked hard for, I'd finally achieved. Sure, I had hiccups along the way, but walking across that stage and knowing that I had a job that would pay me $50,000, starting out, made it all worth it. That was more than anyone in my family had ever made. It felt as if I had arrived. I had achieved my goal.

After years of heartaches and challenges, financial obstacles and perseverance, I could finally support myself and not have to go back and live with my grandmother. I didn't have to do anything. I was on my own. I was independent. To say it was a big relief off my shoulders would be an understatement. I was doing something. I was taking that step into the middle class and, hopefully, working my way up. I marked that moment as the start of my new life.

Little did I know, there would be more twists and turns ahead.

REFLECTION: *What should you take away from this?*

At first, college didn't appear to be worth it. I was always broke, always trying to find a ride each semester from Greenville to Columbia, and struggling to keep everything intact. All my friends had graduated from high school, gotten decent paying jobs, and had cars and money all the time, while I was scraping for pennies to buy textbooks costing more than a hundred dollars. Other college students had more than me as well. They received nice cars, clothes, computers, and whatever they felt they wanted from their parents. During my first semester at the University of South Carolina, I couldn't afford a meal plan. Therefore, I survived that semester on peanut butter and jelly sandwiches, ramen noodles, my monthly Army Reserve checks which were a couple hundred bucks, if not used to buy books and needed supplies, and generous people. When the money disappeared by the end of the month (sometimes sooner), I would surprisingly receive a check from my Aunt Barb or from another unexpected person, a meal from a friend, or a loaned textbook from a classmate so that I could complete my assignment. During my freshman year, I would also catch rides with Tina's family because her older brother attended the University of South Carolina as well.

I wanted to quit and go home. The classes were demanding, and I was struggling to just survive. There were days that I would cry on the inside, keeping a fake smile on my face and not letting a tear exit my eye. There were two things that kept me going: First, I was taught in military basic training to never abandon the mission unless commanded to do so. My mission was to attain my degree in chemical engineering, and I hadn't received a command to quit. Second, I couldn't let myself, or the countless others who believed in me down, especially Grandma. "Pukey, the devil will always test you when you are doing something good," I'd hear her saying in my head. When I would call her each week, I never told her that I was struggling, but she knew and would say different things to keep me encouraged.

The harder things appeared, the harder I worked and prayed. I stopped focusing on graduating and homed in on completing my daily tasks. When my first semester ended, I had achieved a 3.7 GPA. Also, my hard work paid off in other areas, resulting in me getting a high paying Co-Op job during the Spring of 1995, earning a full-tuition scholarship from Carolina Eastman Chemical starting my sophomore year, and purchasing my first car without a cosigner.

At first, the payoff may appear to have been the high paying engineering job after graduation, but I stayed with Fluor Corporation for only six months before joining Southern Company, where I have worked for nearly twenty-two years. When I joined Fluor, the engineering and construction industry was in a slump. Weeks after reporting to work in January 1999, Fluor laid off a third of their workforce. I was not affected and spent my weeks in Philadelphia, supporting a project for a Witco plant being sold to the site management team. In fact, I remember a senior engineer asking why the company hired me then laid off so many people. It was not a good atmosphere.

The reason I left Fluor was because Melanie could not find a decent-paying job for an entry-level civil engineer near me. Graduating a semester behind me, she had applied to numerous companies in Greenville so that she could be with me. We were not married or engaged but had dated for almost three years. Soon, Melanie received an offer from Southern Company to work at Plant Vogtle, a nuclear power plant about forty-five minutes from Melanie's birthplace in Augusta, Georgia. She told the vice president who was recruiting her that she would accept the offer if they considered hiring me. I sent my résumé and cover letter, interviewed a few weeks later, and landed a job that paid slightly less than what I was making at Fluor.

The payoff was more than the compensation and benefits. It was also the satisfaction of seeing the fruits of my labor over the many years, the process taken in the achievement of the goal that continues to benefit me today, the test of my faith during the periods when I wanted to give up, the many diverse friendships developed on my journey, and the fact that Mel and I could start building our life together. I had achieved what a lot of people told me I wouldn't when I first started. Also, my plan to work the rest of my career at Fluor lasted six months because I knew I wanted to marry Melanie. The goal was not to work for Fluor the rest of my life. The goal was to escape poverty and build a better life. And I was doing just that.

APPLICATION: *What can you do to reflect on this lesson as it relates to your life?*

The process for achieving a goal consisted of the following:

1. Identify the real problem or objective. What do you want to achieve long term?

2. How will its outcome affect you?

    a. Visualize what it would be like once you achieved your objective. How would it make you feel? How would you celebrate?

    b. Visualize what failure would look like. How would it affect you and others?

    c. Does the pleasure of achieving your goal outweigh the pain of failure?

    d. Internalize your answers because you will have to draw on these feelings when you face obstacles.

3. Break your long-term objective into short-term tasks. Don't get discouraged if you do not know all the tasks. For example, if your goal is to attend college and you are a ninth grader, do the following:

    a. Improve your grades. Your GPA over the course of your entire time in high school plays a huge part in whether colleges will accept your application.

    b. Don't be afraid to ask for help. Befriend the smart students. Talk to your teachers. Attend tutoring sessions. Remember, you can't get anything for nothing.

    c. Meet with your guidance counselor and express your interest in going to college. Also, tell your teachers and ask for their help. This may also involve doing extra credit work. Note: They may not take you seriously at first, or they may discourage you or redirect you to a technical trade. Stick to your goals, and visit them numerous times until you convince them to support you.

d. If you are successful in improving your grades to A's and B's, then talk to your teacher and guidance counselor about taking college preparation and Advanced Placement courses. These courses are harder and will test your resolve. In some cases, grades from these classes count more toward your GPA.

e. Start preparing for the SAT and/or ACT exams. The SAT exam is a three-plus hour multiple choice exam comprised of two sections: Evidence-Based Reading and Writing and Math. Please take the exam seriously by studying and taking many practice tests before taking the actual exam because colleges use your score to see if you qualify for admittance. Talk to your counselor about available SAT prep courses. They may tell you that most students start preparing near the end of their sophomore year. But you are not most students. After you are consistently scoring high on the practice tests, sign up for the test. The average SAT score in 2020 is 1060. You should strive to meet or exceed the average.

f. Get involved in extracurricular activities like sports, student government, or community service.

g. Work with your counselor to determine possible career paths and college majors. Research potential salaries and required education for each career path. The Google search engine is a great starting place. Will your chosen career path help you meet your goals or bundle you with a huge amount of debt? Is there a lot of competition in the field? How is the job market?

    h. Research and apply for colleges that offer your chosen major as early as possible, typically early in your senior year.

    i. Research and apply for financial aid and scholarships.

    j. Choose the best college that provides you the greatest potential for success (low cost, high post-college job placement, great professors, faster payback, etc.).

4. Identify the players.

    a. Who is on your team? Do they want you to succeed? Can you trust them? What do they have to gain from your success or lose from your failure? Who do you need to recruit to the team?

    b. Who are your opponents? What do they have to gain from your failure or lose from your success? What do you need from them to be successful? Believe it or not, these people could be friends or family members who love you as long as you are in the same boat with them, but despise you when you have more than them. Love them, but know that they may not understand your vision until weeks after its fulfillment.

    c. Has anyone done it before? What can you learn from them? What were their successes and failures? What lessons did they learn?

5. Assign deadlines to each task, and develop a schedule. In Stephen Covey's great book, *The Seven Habits of Highly Effective People*, he states that you should "begin with the end in mind." Decide when you need to achieve your

objective, then work your way backwards, assigning deadlines for each task. For example, let's use the first item on the previous example above: improve your grades.

    a. Review your syllabus and determine how many points are needed for an A.

    b. Identify the easy points. For some courses, you receive points for attendance, class participation, and homework. You should attain all these points because they may make the small difference needed should you score lower than expected on a test or quiz.

    c. Quizzes, exams and projects are the next areas of focus. Determine what it will take to get a high grade. Start preparing for them as early as possible. What do you need to study? Who can help you? For projects with future deadlines, do a little bit of it each day or as much as possible today. Then spend the remaining time reviewing and improving your work before the due date.

    d. Ask your teacher for extra-credit assignments.

    e. Develop a great relationship with the teacher. That relationship can be the difference between an A or B when your grades are borderline.

6. Passionately drive to completion. Always ask yourself what can you do at this moment to move you one step closer to your objective. Be aware of the vision, but focus your efforts on the successful completion of the daily tasks.

7. Celebrate the small wins and learn from the failures along the way.

CAVIAR TIME

Go to your private space or find a new one. Close and lock the door. Stare at yourself in the mirror. Repeat these words:

"Wow. My blood, sweat, and tears have paid off. I am extremely thankful. There were so many times that I wanted to quit and take the easier path. But I pressed on when I was tired, hurt, or discouraged.

I realize that I have not done this on my own. *So* many people have helped me. Although I cannot afford to repay them - none of them would accept payment if I tried, I will pay it forward by encouraging others to achieve their dreams.

Though my journey is not over, I realize that I have all that I need to be successful. I am smart. I am handsome/beautiful. I know how to gain the skills that I don't possess. The scars of my past, both emotional and physical, have become my impenetrable armor.

I cannot explain a lot of things that have happened to me. Unexpected and unrequested aid arrive at my time of need, tense encounters miraculously diffuse overnight without my involvement, and heavenly oversight has been sent at times I was being reckless. There are so many traps. Avoiding pregnancies, diseases, arrests, fights, expulsions, and fines are challenging, especially when society expects that from you. How am I alive, free, and living well today? Thank you, God!"

PROFESSIONAL TIDBIT

Time and time again, I have witnessed young professionals, shortly after graduating and getting that first job, buy a new truck, car, boat, or home. When I ask them why, they respond that they deserve it and can afford the payments (with no mention of the principal, term, or interest).

Do you remember Ryan's story from earlier? Hypothetically, let's consider his payment obligations after his wife quit her job:

Ryan's Salary = $7,083/month ($85,000)

Item	Monthly Payment
Car loan payment (two new cars)	$750 (total)
Home mortgage	$1,100
Credit card debt for wedding (min payment)	$100
Benefits, 401(k), and taxes (federal, state, property, etc.)	$2,433
Food (add more for full family)	$600
Home maintenance (i.e., yard, repairs)	$200
Car maintenance (i.e. fuel, oil changes, tires, repairs)	$592
Bills and utilities	$707
Health and fitness	$50
Church and charities	$100
Shopping	$100
Insurances (life, auto, liability, etc.)	$240
Net income (leftover money)	**$111**

Suppose that Ryan purchased mediocre cars and donated one percent to church and charity. Ryan and his wife would have $111 remaining each month. This had to be a shock to their lifestyle after removing his wife's nearly $100,000 salary.

Now let's analyze this another way:

Item	Commitment
Two new cars (cars last 7-10 years)	5 years per car
Home mortgage	15–30 years
Credit card debt for wedding (minimum payment)	30 years or more
Benefits, 401K, and taxes (federal, state, property, etc.)	Permanent
Food	Grows with family
Home maintenance (i.e., yard, repairs)	Permanent
Car maintenance (i.e. oil changes, tires, repairs)	Permanent
Bills and utilities	Permanent
Health and fitness	Permanent
Church and charities	Permanent
Shopping	Permanent
Insurances (auto, home, liability, etc.)	Permanent

What if Ryan did not like his job? Can he take a few months off to find a new one? What if he receives a crazy assignment? Can he refuse it, knowing that it may stifle future growth and promotion?

Eric Tyson's *Personal Finance for Dummies* and *Investing for Dummies* are great books about maintaining and growing your personal wealth. Eric explains how everyone should use software like Quicken and Mint to track their finances weekly and develop a budget. He also explains that you should make your investments automatic so that you can save for retirement, plan for a big purchase, or add another income stream.

Wealth is more than money. It is having the freedom to make choices that you want to make versus those that you must make. Wealth is also time, a commodity you cannot get back.

One of my fellow chemical engineering graduates has not worked for anyone for more than fifteen years. The book that I will introduce in the next professional tidbit changed his and his wife's (also a chemical engineer) lives forever. They are one of the couples we vacation with every year.

Life is Short. Live it Well.

I did not have a heart attack,
but I wasn't so sure at the time.

In 2010, I worked at a coal-fired power generation plant in Cartersville, Georgia. Each day brought more and more stress. I worked for a difficult boss. Some might say he was biased. In fact, older white male employees would tell me that they were ashamed of how my boss treated me. I won't characterize him that way, but I will say that by examining the way he treated me at times, it could appear that way.

Imagine your supervisor sitting in a meeting with your whole team. Due to the size and shape of the room, I sat behind him. When he would address me, he would do so without ever turning to face me, or even swiveling his body in my direction. He'd just talk to me from the back of his head.

It's difficult to imagine, and yet, that's the way it was.

That was disrespectful, but that wasn't the whole story. I would assign projects and tasks to my team, and sometimes this boss would change the job without letting me know. For instance, if I had somebody working on something, he'd talk to them and change the scope including stopping work before tasks were completed, leaving me in the dark. This effect was amplified by the fact that I had a limited budget, and a schedule to meet to avoid delaying plant startup after a planned maintenance outage. To further put this in perspective, each day that the plant was not running cost the company over $1 million. It felt like he did everything in his power to make me fail. He did not succeed, but I think he gave it his best shot.

We were working on a $1.2 billion Scrubber project, environmental control equipment that converted sulfur dioxide found in plant stack emissions into wallboard quality gypsum. Although I was the chemical process engineer, I found myself making all the critical decisions. I helped form and train the team; developed and managed the multimillion-dollar budget to within less than one percent variance each month; communicated the vision to company executives, senators, and external organizations; led the startup and commissioning of the equipment as part of the plant operations; and planned and coordinated the outage maintenance work inside the vessels, just to name a few of my responsibilities. In fact, my boss's peer at another plant commented one time that he should send me to the cross-company management meetings since I was the one with all the answers.

One day, a compliance manager position was posted to the internal job listing board. Everyone close to me, and myself, knew that was my job. Who else knew how the environmental controls performed and could communicate technical information in a way that a fifth grader could understand? Also, I was great with people. There was no one else onsite who could influence the entire plant population to move to action like I did. And I did all of that without a lick of authority. I simply treated people with respect, taking time to teach and assist them when needed, expressing the importance of the project, attaining their buy-in, and recognizing them for their accomplishments in helping us achieve our objectives.

I applied, then waited. A few weeks later, I received a notification that they did not receive enough qualified candidates, but that I remained in the candidate pool. Days passed, then weeks. Until one day, my friend Gary asked, "What is your interview time?" *My interview time?* I thought. I had not received any notification of being selected for an interview or of being rejected. In fact, I received a rejection letter twenty-one days after they announced the successful candidate. It turns out that the plant manager had called the successful candidate and asked him to apply after receiving the first candidate pool. This would have been okay if the precedent had not been that unsuccessful internal candidates were notified before the interview and were provided feedback.

I was hurt. All the hours, nights, weekends, and holidays worked were no longer meaningful. All the presentations in which I convinced the CEOs, boards of directors, public service commission, senators, and others that the billion-dollar investment was in capable hands, were worthless. Constructive feedback, or any feedback, would have helped ease the pain of rejection. But there was none.

I contemplated leaving the company, but quickly realized that the corporation was not just one or a few persons, and the grass was not always greener on the other side. I had built a wonderful career, supported by a diverse network, in a short period of time and was not going to let one person deter me. Also, my peers and I strongly believed in our corporate values: unquestionable trust, superior performance, and total commitment.

So, instead, I decided to take a stand. I was going to stop doing my boss's job. He had to make the critical decisions instead of me. Besides, he was earning a lot more. I continued to smile and treat people with respect. I continued to bust my butt on the job. However, the one or two times that I pushed back on the decision-making did not end well. Suddenly in management's eyes, I went from being a top performer to an angry black male overnight. In fact, my boss and another manager, also a white male, pulled me into my boss's office and said that I was "maliciously obedient." What is that? Those two words don't go together.

There had been times in my life that I realized that I needed to back down, even if I had not done anything wrong. That I had to smile and play along until the conditions improved, and understand that I was fighting a losing battle. And that is what I did. Needless to say, I became a top performer again and received two generous cash awards.

I worked hard and played the part while also successfully completing the multiyear project. During this time, I turned down opportunities for career advancement because I had promised the boss who had treated me so badly that I would not abandon him until the completion of the project. After fulfilling my promise, I convinced the plant management to allow me to shadow the corporate environmental affairs department for three months on the plant's dime. It was a win-win, especially for the environmental affairs department, which received free labor. Upon my arrival, I worked extremely hard and, in no time, was producing just as much, or better, than their full-time staff. The three-month term was extended to six months, then nine months, and eventually I landed a full-time role in that department.

Things were challenging at work, and unfortunately, I didn't have much relief at home. While all of that was going on, I was also experiencing a rocky patch in my marriage. For various reasons, we weren't seeing eye to eye on things and were starting to grow apart.

One day, I was at work and began having chest pains. I didn't really put two and two together and kept working, ignoring the pain. On the way home, the pain got worse. My wife tried to talk me into seeing a doctor, but I refused. "No," I said. "It's nothing."

Finally, when I got home it got really bad with my chest feeling like it was going to explode. She took me to Prompt Care. They took my vitals and ran some tests. The next thing I knew, I was in the back of an ambulance going to the hospital.

I got to the Emergency Room, and they ran an EKG or electrocardiogram. Every time your heart beats, an electrical signal travels through the heart. An EKG measures those electrical signals. "You're about to have a heart attack," they said. I'm not sure if anyone has ever said that to you, but hearing the words can certainly make your heart skip a beat. As it was, another doctor reviewed the results and determined I was not having a heart attack. Instead, I had a slow heart rate, coupled with what appeared to be an irregular heartbeat. Or so he thought. I was admitted to the hospital for further testing and stayed there for two nights while doctors ran a whole battery of tests to be sure.

That was a lonely time. I was scared because I had no idea what was going on or how it would turn out. I had to face those moments by myself for the most part. My kids were young, so my wife was home with them. This gave me a lot of time to think, reflect on my life, and consider all the decisions I had made up until that point.

High on my list was writing a book. I strongly believe everybody has a purpose. I feel a responsibility to share my story with others who may need a little encouragement to keep going on their chosen path. At that time in the hospital, I kept thinking, "I'm going to finish my book, finish my book. I have a book."

That was one thing I thought about. I also reflected on how I treated people. Usually I'm very nice to people, but I asked myself, "Could I have treated people better? Did I take time to listen?" My wife would sometimes say that I don't listen well. "Could I be a better listener with her? Have I done right by my kids? Am I raising them right?" I'll admit, I was probably extremely hard on my older son. I focused on discipline, discipline, discipline—a lot more than with my younger son. I wondered if I was too hard on him. Those are the types of thoughts I had. "Are they going to be taken care of? Who would come in and replace me? Would he give them the same love I would?"

Spending two days face-to-face with your own mortality will certainly give you a new perspective on things. I had come a long way from the boy back at Woodland-Pearce Homes. I saw that I hadn't come as far as I wanted in a few fronts. God gave me that time alone to sit with the truth so I could be more careful in my next steps. If I got out, that's what I would do.

Ultimately, the doctors determined I did not have a heart attack, but I did have a great deal of stress. They gave me some highly concentrated aspirin, and they advised me to exercise and relax more. Although I was discharged without needing surgery, I did leave with a change of heart.

After that experience, I stopped taking some things seriously. I used to stress about the smallest things, then I realized life was just too short for that.

My wife and I signed up for a twelve-week business course sponsored by our church, Word of Faith Cathedral in Austell, Georgia. They brought in experts and facilitators to guide us through creating each section of the business plan. Each week we learned something new and then applied it to complete the next section. We developed a business plan, then formulated an exit plan for her to quit her full-time job and become an entrepreneur.

We got our finances in order and took the leap. She now owns A Little Slice of Heaven Bakery in Decatur *with five employees. I feel as though we have grown closer. Prior to that experience, I would've

---

* www.ALSHBakery.com

been much more reticent to go for it. I would've said "No, we gotta have a couple million dollars in the bank before we try this."

After my stint in the hospital, I knew if you have an opportunity to go for your dream, just go for it. There's no time like the present; tomorrow is *not* promised.

REFLECTION: *What should you take away from this?*

Stress has always been a part of my life. In fact, I would argue that a certain level of stress is good for you. However, this was the first time that it had affected my health.

As I've grown older, my responsibilities at work and home have increased. Of course, I've earned more money, but money is not everything. In hindsight, I spent more and more time chasing the next promotion, fulfilling my duties as a husband and father, and researching investments that would allow me to retire early. I neglected time for exercise, relaxation, and reflection, which are also vital for a vibrant life.

Today, I focus more on removing obstacles for others, encouraging my teams to improve and do more, celebrating their accomplishments along the way, and delivering optimistic outcomes before everyone else sees it. I strongly believe that teams can create their own outcomes by performing enough due diligence and hard work. In addition to my duties at work, I am also helping my wife run her bakery. In my spare time, I serve as the chief financial officer, chief technical officer, and human resources vice president, while allowing her to make her own decisions as to how the business should be run. I also help my boys with their homework, sports, and other needs. My friends will tell you that I am always busy.

I do all of this while exercising each day, playing basketball weekly, taking time each day to play *Call of Duty* with my friends in Texas and Charleston, and vacationing at least a week each year. Life is too short.

APPLICATION: *What can you do to reflect on this lesson as it relates to your life?*

According to the American Heart Association, heart disease is the number one health risk for all Americans. Here are a few ways to avoid it:

1. Exercise at least five days per week. An hour in the gym each day that includes at least fifteen minutes of cardio will do wonders for your heart.

2. Eat healthy. Eating a diet high in saturated fats, trans fat, and cholesterol has been linked to heart disease and related conditions.

3. Work hard, play harder. Take time weekly to do things that you enjoy. I enjoy playing basketball and hanging out with the fellas. During those times, I do not think about goals or work.

4. Take time to relax. My family and I enjoy fishing and watching movies. Recently, my wife and I introduced our sons to *Oliver* (1968), *The Sound of Music* (1965), *Annie* (1982) and *Les Misérables* (2012)—all classic musicals. Surprisingly, they enjoyed them as much as we did.

5. Stay focused on goals, but be flexible. Only focus your efforts on one to two goals at a time. The path to your goal is not always a straight line. You may fail multiple times or even move backward before you achieve your objective.

CAVIAR TIME

Go to your private space or find a new one. Close and lock the door. Stare at yourself in the mirror. Repeat these words:

"God, I have proven to society that I belong. I have taken all their punches and insults and converted them into positive energy. Yet, they still test me. Still insult me. Still mistreat me. Still ignore me.

Life continues to be a constant test of my faith in people, religion, government, and self. But I have faith in YOU. You have gotten me this far, and I know You have great plans for me. Honestly, the little games that people play now are not as serious as the life-threatening ones growing up. No fists, knives, guns, or extreme emotions are involved.

Regardless of how people treat me, I will treat them with respect and love. I will give more than what is expected of me on my job, sports or other activities that I am involved in. I will influence and support people in achieving their goals because I know what you have brought me through. I will take time to exercise, relax, and celebrate the journey with my loved ones because life is precious and time is limited. I will take, and enjoy, the high road!"

PROFESSIONAL TIDBIT

Whether you love your job or not, you should always prepare for an emergency or life-changing event. Taking this one step further, you should plan for a future layoff, manager change, or pay reduction. Since you are living opposite of the "Welfare Cheese Mindset," those seem like unlikely events. However, study the financial crisis of 2007 or 2008, the COVID-19 pandemic of 2020, or the Great Depression during the 1930s.

Don't rush to build a bunker in your backyard and stack it with canned goods. Instead, read books about personal finance, investing, and business. Establish an emergency fund with at least 6 months of expenses. Slowly develop other income streams (arrows flowing into your box).

In the last chapter, I introduced a couple that I admire quite a bit. Their names are Rodney and Kellee. We were in the same chemical engineering graduating class. Kellee was extremely smart, a 4.0 GPA chemical engineering student. Rodney was smart as well. Upon graduating, they both went to work for ExxonMobil in Houston, Texas.

In 2002, Kellee and Rodney, Eulah and Mike (also graduates of the University of South Carolina), and my wife and I and took our first vacation together in Jamaica. Not only did we have fun exploring the resort, participating in excursions, and relaxing by the pool and beach, we discussed family, career, and future. We had such a great time that we have vacationed together every year since.

During one of those early vacations, I introduced Robert Kiyosaki's *Rich Dad Poor Dad: What the Rich Teach Their Kids about Money That the Poor and Middle Class Do Not!* That book changed our lives. We all started buying rental properties. While I have since exited that space, the remaining two couples are still investing. But Kellee and Rodney took it to another level, allowing Rodney to leave his job after a few years, pay off the debt on their rental properties, and travel around the world.

From time to time, I would find similar books, like Lee Jenkins' *Taking Care of Business: Establishing a Financial Legacy for the African American Family*, and share them with my friends. Lee's book moved me so much that I purchased ten copies and shipped them to my closest friends. Rodney introduced George Clason's *The Richest Man in Babylon* to us.

Earn a great living while on the job but build wealth in your spare time.

Sharpen Your Focus

When your motivation or focus is low, help someone else achieve their goals.

I've always prided myself on living in the future. I had to, just to be able to see beyond my childhood circumstances and imagine myself somewhere different and better. That doesn't mean I don't appreciate life day by day, but it does mean my eyes are firmly forward, not gazing at the ground or feeling stuck. It means planning and thinking about the next step.

Envisioning the future, the single most important goal in my life right now is trying to help my wife achieve her dream. She had a dream of owning her own bakery, so after working eighteen years for a major corporation, she resigned in May 2017. She has worked extremely hard and has a passion that is unmatched. In 2018, she competed on the Food Network as part of the *Winner Cakes All* series. Our efforts have been focused on making that a reality without breaking the bank. In January 2019, we made her dream a reality by purchasing an established bakery in Decatur, Georgia.

That has entailed throwing all my resources—time, money, knowledge, love, whatever I have—into that dream. It's been challenging in

2020 during the COVID-19 pandemic especially when your employees leave temporarily because they can make more money from unemployment checks than they can at work. Running a business is pretty much like having another child. You have to really nurture it, feed it, and raise it for it to be successful. As a business owner, you are accountable for your customers, employees, and the communities that you serve. We're heading in the right direction, and one of the things I pray for now is the resolve to continue and not give up. That's the single most important goal that I'm working on at this moment.

Focus has been one of my keys to success, and I'll admit, I didn't have the right focus for a period of time. I was moving in my direction, and my wife was moving in her direction. It came to a point where I felt like I would have to either slow down and align my direction with hers or risk us going too far in opposite directions, potentially causing us to end our marriage. Ultimately, I chose to change my focus from myself to my family. Now I'm wholly focused on my wife's business.

Reflecting on my life so far, I have achieved everything I wanted to achieve. I wanted to go to college, and I went to college, leaving with Chemical Engineering and Master of Business Administration degrees. I wanted to be debt-free, and I've been debt free twice. I wanted to get married, and I've been married since 2001. I wanted to have two healthy boys, and I have two healthy, intelligent, handsome boys. At work, I wanted to achieve a management position with good pay, and I've achieved it. Everything I've wanted and set goals to achieve, I've done.

I still found myself in an interesting position. I lost that fire, stopped setting goals, and got complacent in my achievement. I was moving in my own direction, but I wasn't exactly going anywhere. I was like a hamster, spinning on a wheel. I said I wanted to achieve other things, but I was not really determined to do them, nor was I focused on success.

When my wife decided to go after her dream, it reawakened that determined goal-seeker. So much so that I applied and attained a great position at our gas subsidiary. For now, my passion is invested in her success and building my reputation at my company's gas subsidiary. Her victory will be our victory.

Growing this business helped me clarify and recommit to my next goal, which is to become financially free. Debt-free is nice, but I can't walk away from my job and still be able to provide for my family. Having a job that I now enjoy is a huge plus. I can put food on the table and ensure the kids have a quality education.

That's a pretty challenging prospect, now that we're down to just one income and investing in the business. That makes this the most important goal in my life right now as there is now a lot more at stake. Right now, I have a slight fear of failure; if something goes wrong and I lose my job, I would not be able to support my family in the way I have been thus far. I also have doubt, wondering if I still have it in me to go this path. But I had these same doubts when I finished high school. By acknowledging that, I was able to get what I needed, and give my all to my dreams.

Fear of failure and doubt are my current inner demons. This goal is a challenge, and I never shy away from a challenge.

REFLECTION: *What should you take away from this?*

There have been many times that I have lost that push to move forward. Before college, I would often succumb to the pressures of being poor and rejected by society. No one seemed to like poor, black boys. Some feared me and others just downright hated me. Why would it take eight police cars to pull over three young boys riding bicycles one night to see a girl? Why would the Jump-Out Boys raid my neighbor's home in broad daylight with guns drawn, while me and my cousins were playing in the front yard? Why did it feel like I was constantly being harassed or taunted to do something wrong?

Fortunately, I was surrounded by great people like Grandma, Aunt Barb, Cousin Val, my closest friends, kind teachers, and other people who saw my potential. They would always say the right thing to reignite that fire. When they were not around, music from rap artists like NWA, Ice Cube, LL Cool J, Geto Boys, MC Hammer, Tupac, Jay Z, Biggie, and others would fill the void. Sounds strange, but their lyrics spoke to the pain and anger that I felt. I also learned to turn my anger and frustration into action. The more people who called me a failure, turned their noses up at me, or picked at the clothes I wore, the more I studied.

That changed after I entered the military. Although I still loved my music, I was self-motivated and not bothered by the opinions of others. If the US Army could not break me physically or mentally, then a civilian was not going to stop me. Anger and frustration were replaced by discipline, honor, courage, leadership, and teamwork as my drivers for achieving success. Attaining a Chemical Engineering degree was not easy by any means. I will forever be grateful to the US Army for equipping me mentally, physically, and financially.

Last, I lost the fire to achieve financial freedom. I was debt-free, had a great family, was living below my means, and had achieved my career goal. Becoming financially free was a long-term goal and I had not set any short-term goals. I got complacent, and everything in my life started to suffer. To combat this, I adopted my wife's dream and fed off her passion for its attainment. Before you know it, I was back on track.

APPLICATION: *What can you do to reflect on this lesson as it relates to your life?*

From time to time, you will lose focus or the energy to push forward. This may be the result of harsh words received from someone you trust, failure on a test or objective, the loss of a loved one, or simply mental or physical exhaustion. Don't panic. You're human.

During those periods, take some time to relax and reflect on your life. Are you on the right path? What motivates or discourages you? Is there something or someone standing in your way? Warning! This will sound weird. Help someone achieve their goal. Tutor a friend or stranger. God tends to bless people who bless his children.

CAVIAR TIME

Go to your private space or find a new one. Close and lock the door. Stare at yourself in the mirror. Repeat these words:

"Relax. I have achieved more than I would have ever dreamed before. Have I celebrated my achievements along the way? (Smile.) I will celebrate them now.

Reflect. What is my purpose? What am I doing now to achieve it? What is driving me? Have I steered off course?

Renew. Who can I help achieve their goals? My spouse? My children? My friends? My coworkers? Or a random stranger?

Restart. I am back on track. Helping others has reinvigorated me. God is great!"

PROFESSIONAL TIDBIT

Career setbacks can come unexpectedly. You can be passed over for a promotion, receive a different manager, or be affected by changing business conditions. And this can happen when you are performing at the top of your game, exceeding everyone's expectations. I have had my share of setbacks. Some of them were caused by my "Welfare Cheese Mindset." Here are a few:

1. **Networking** - Being an introvert early in my career, I focused on my performance. And I was good. One of my Leadership Development peers told me that I should schedule meetings with upper managers and express my interest in management positions. I smiled but chose to focus on delivering superior results instead. Result: he is a politically savvy vice president and I am a talented program manager.

2. **Manager Change** - I was performing at a high level in a position that the company had created for me. I was untouchable, or so I thought. Then my manager received a promotion. The next manager was good but was soon replaced by a young manager who had failed in a previous department management role. Friends who had worked for this person told me that I should find another job. But I felt that my superior performance and unmatched client support could overcome anything. Result: the manager was one of the worst ones I have ever had. Thankfully, I moved on to a better job in a different subsidiary. Ironically, the manager was promoted.

3. **Sensitive** - After being removed from the Leadership Development program, I decided that upper management was not for me. I chose to focus on delivering results and helping my peers achieve their

career aspirations. My friend (who was also a plant manager) told me that I should meet with my old plant manager, apologize for any misconceptions, and seek constructive feedback. Ignoring his advice, because I felt I had not done anything wrong, my career was stagnant for a few years. I constantly interviewed but never successfully landed the job. Finally, I scheduled a lunch meeting with that plant manager. To my surprise, he sang my praises and offered his support. Result: soon after, I was back on track, receiving a management promotion.

You must always fight complacency and inflated egos. You also need to understand your worth and consistently work on your career. During my recent setback, I read Dr. Karen Gurney's *Stacked: Double Your Job Interviews, Leverage Recruiters, Unlock LinkedIn** based on a recommendation from one of my best friends, Ernie. That recommendation was a godsend. I enjoyed Dr. Gurney's book so much that I hired her to help me find another job. She helped me assess my career worth, she revised my résumé and LinkedIn profile, and she applied for jobs on my behalf and helped me prepare for the interviews. As a result, I received two job offers (one internal and one external) in a matter of weeks. The job that I accepted was my dream job. Karen has also helped two of my friends find great jobs.

When you face adversity on your job, first evaluate yourself. Do not beat yourself down and devalue your capabilities, however. Are you meeting the expectations set at the beginning of the year? If you are, then work with someone like Karen to help you assess your value. Karen was expensive, but my friends and I agree that it was one of the greatest investments in our career.

Every great change in my life was preceded by a low point.

---

* https://hire-a-headhunter.com. https://karengurney.com

Loss

*When experiencing a loss, allow emotions
to run their course so that success can
take the baton to the finish line.*

I think the lowest point in my life so far has been the loss of my grandmother. I'm the oldest of four boys. My brother is two years younger than I am, and the other two are a year apart. Growing up, they always had their dads around. Mine was never around, and I always felt like the outcast. Whenever they got in trouble, I got in trouble. Whenever I got in trouble, I got in trouble.

Unbeknownst to me, when I was a child, my grandmother told my great aunt, Eulah Brunston, "Frances is out there running around with all those men. I'm going to take care of Pukey. Pukey's going to be okay."

Frances is my mother's middle name, and Pukey is me. I never knew that until after Grandma passed, but she was always there when I was growing up. Anytime I got in trouble, no matter what, she would come over and visit. She would always grab me, and we'd go to the laundromat and fold clothes. She'd pay me a little change or a dollar or two. It wouldn't be much, but it was great. I just enjoyed being with her, enjoyed being around her.

When she got older, there wasn't anybody to look after her. That's when they asked me to go move in with her. So I'd been with her since I was fourteen years old. It was just me and Grandma. When she finally passed, I felt a lot of regret because I had always said I was gonna one day write a book and be able to say, "Hey, Grandma, I finally did it. I finally did something." She'd already said that I'd done a number of things for the family, but I just wanted to have something that I did to benefit others.

In her final days, I took off a week or so just to be with her there. Staying in the hospital room with her and watching her suffer was a painful experience. The first night I cried the entire night. I could not sleep. I listened for every breath just to make sure she was okay. I'd get up to make sure she was fine. The nurses came in and moved her around just to help make her comfortable. I felt helpless. There was nothing else I could do but be with her and cry.

Finally, she sent me away. "You gotta go take care of your wife and your boys, Pukey" she said. "I'm going to be okay." My aunt and uncle were there also, so we took turns. I'd drive two and a half hours to check on the family and come back to be with her the next day.

Then, one night, my aunt stayed overnight with her, while I went to my mom's house to get some rest. Only a few hours after I left the hospital, I got the call from Aunt Barb that Grandma had passed. I thought Grandma wanted to give me a break, but she really needed me to go so she could make her transition. It was hard. She was ninety-two years old, and she lived a great life.

One thing I regret is spending less time with her as I got older. Growing up, we were always together, but after I got married and started having kids, I would visit much less often. I didn't visit her enough or spend enough time with her. So even though there were many things I've done for her over the years, I regret that.

I celebrated her as much as I could. Once, we had a surprise party for her, and eighty people showed up. It was all about her. She really enjoyed that. The celebrations were important, but I could've spent more one-on-one time. There was a lot more I could have learned from her if I had just taken the time to sit down with her, or even interview her. But I didn't do it, so I'll just have to deal with it.

She lived a good life. She was a strong woman. My rock. I saw her go through so much, and I wanted to be that one person who didn't put her through so much hell. I wanted to be the bright candle. The person she could say she was proud of.

I shared this on Facebook after she passed:

On December 28, 2017 we buried a great woman. When I was fourteen years of age, I moved in with my grandmother. I lived with her until I graduated from college. I learned so much from Grandma. As a teenager, I thought my life was hard and would look for someone to blame. My grandma taught me to create my own future, even if I didn't know how to get there. She taught me to treat EVERYONE with respect and love because you didn't know what angel God was going to send to help you. Also, she taught me to treasure family and friends. Observing Grandma during that period in my life, I matured beyond my years. We celebrated her multiple times while she was living, but I could never repay her. She wouldn't have accepted it if I tried. :) In closing, I am thankful for having her for ninety-two blessed years (forty-two for me). If your grandmother, mother, great aunt, etc. is still living, call and tell them that you love them. Visit and cherish them while you can.

REFLECTION: *What should you take away from this?*

Rather than sharing my personal reflection, I am going to share a poem that I wrote about my grandma. To write it, I interviewed her siblings, children, and others. She was an extraordinary woman, but I will let you be the judge of that.

Who Is That Strong Woman

Who is that strong woman
That has had many titles?
To her employers, she was a housekeeper,
nanny, cook, cotton picker, and parent.
But for her family, she was a doctor, chef, counselor,
mediator, motivator, psychiatrist, and much more.
Who is that strong woman?

Who is that strong woman
That lived in a house infested with rats and roaches,
But cleaned large houses in affluent neighborhoods?
At times, her measly, out-of-pocket, housekeeping wages
were not enough to pay the rent or all of the bills;
Yet, she kept a place for us to stay, the
lights on, and food on the table.
Who is that strong woman?

Who is that strong woman
That alone raised eight children, eighteen
grandchildren, and twelve great-grandchildren?
With the exception of a few, all of them have
been successful in some fashion or another.
She has generated a nurse, truck driver, clinical therapist,
chemical engineer, X-ray technician, a pool of chefs,
janitor, barber, assistant manager, and many more.
Who is that strong woman?

Who is that strong woman
That was forced to be a tough woman at a young age?
As a child, she was punished because she
would not stand up to a guy bully.
In fact, she was told that she would continually
be punished for the same outcome,
The next day, she fought back by ramming
the guy's head into some cow manure.
Who is that strong woman?

Who is that strong woman
That would go to the ends of the Earth for her family?
During a time where the Knight Riders
in white sheets terrorized the streets,
She would walk alone miles in the dark to work.
How could a woman be so fearless?
Who is that strong woman?

Who is that strong woman
Who always placed her family's well-
being before her own?
When her kids got in trouble, she would
always be there to rescue them if possible.
When she couldn't, she would fall on her knees and pray,
Her strong relationship with God has
watched over all of her kids
Who is that strong woman?

Who is that strong woman
Who has only cried three times in twenty-nine years?
She lost her oldest daughter to a heart attack, youngest
child to drugs, and her mother to old age,
But she cried away her pain and
sorrow for each momentarily,
then stood tall for her family.
Who is that strong woman?

Who is that strong woman
That is slowly approaching eighty years of age,
But continues to cook, run errands, and
care for people her age and older?
Actually, she has done this her entire life,
How could her heart be filled with
that much love for people?
Who is that strong woman?

Who is that strong woman
Who walks gracefully and without fear,
But has the power to discipline you with a simple stare?
She had sons that would constantly fight,
a grandson who almost burned the house down,
and daughters who would stay out late into the night;
Yet all of them graduated from high school.
Who is that strong woman?

That woman is my grandmother, Rosa Mae Wideman,
And she represents millions of women of her time.
These women believed in building strong
families and attending church.
There was nothing they wouldn't do for their families.
Take the time now and visit your mother,
grandmother, or great-grandmother.
Tell them that you love them and how much you care,
Because when they are gone, you can't get them back.

APPLICATION: *What can you do to reflect on this lesson as it relates to your life?*

Take time to honor your parents, grandparents, and other relatives who paved the way for you. If they are living, then you are truly blessed. They have so many experiences that will help you. Interview them. Study your family history. Participate in planning a family reunion.

If you experience a loss, like I did, allow yourself time to mourn. Men, do not be afraid to cry. Women, do not apologize for your feelings. This is healthy. Be careful who you share your feelings with, especially those at work. During my grief, I shared my feelings with a plant manager and friend. Later, I learned that he told everyone that I was a drama queen. This really hurt me and permanently damaged that relationship. Needless to say, he is no longer plant manager. As Grandma would say, "God has a way of dealing with ugly."

Only time heals. Therefore, allow your grieving time to run its course. You will bounce back stronger than ever. The best way to honor your loved one and their memories is for you to live your best life and help your relatives do the same.

CAVIAR TIME

Go to your private space or find a new one. Close and lock the door. Stare at yourself in the mirror. Repeat these words:

"Why now? Why couldn't I have just one more year, month, or day? Why didn't I spend more time? Why didn't I do more?

The times that we had were special. I will refer to those memories in my time of grief. And I understand that my grieving is a long process filled with emotions that must run their course.

The best thing I can do is press on toward my goals, because that is what my loved one would have wanted. I will love more, smile more, and laugh more. I know that my loved one is smiling down on me from heaven. God, watch over me and my family during our time of bereavement!"

PROFESSIONAL TIDBIT

Although we want our loved ones to live happily forever, one or more of them may die unexpectedly. It can be the result of a car accident, bad health, a pandemic, suicide, a crime, or simply old age. Even if we anticipate it, we cannot predict how we will respond.

During my grandma's last days in the hospital, I observed that grief affects people differently. Some relatives were sad that this matriarch who held this family together for decades was finally meeting her end. They could not let her go and insisted that the family invest whatever costs to keep Grandma alive on a machine. Others had feelings of regret. They felt that they could have visited Grandma more and possibly helped prolong her life. Some relatives were angry. Rather than deal with their emotions, they got wasted and wanted to fight other relatives. A handful of us kept a level head, at least when others were around.

When it was just me and Grandma, I wept like a baby. During those periods of weakness, I emailed some friends, including some coworkers. Most of them were true friends who cared for me and offered their sympathy and support. One of them told others that I was a drama queen. *Really?*

The loss of a loved one is life's most stressful event and can cause a major emotional crisis. You may not be prepared for the intensity and duration of your emotions or how swiftly your moods may change. You may even begin to doubt the stability of your mental health. But be assured that these feelings are healthy and appropriate and will help you come to terms with your loss. It takes time to fully absorb the impact of a major loss. You never stop missing your loved one, but the pain eases after time and allows you to go on with your life.

Be careful with what you share with your coworkers, especially during periods of weakness.

The Mental Health America* website offers advice on how to help others deal with loss. They are as follows:

1. Allow them to share their feelings. This is therapeutic and helps them make sense of their emotions.

2. Don't offer false support by saying "it was for the best." How do you know? Are you God?

3. Offer practical help. Volunteer to babysit or perform their work tasks or other errands to save them time.

4. Be patient. It will take them time to work through their feelings.

5. Encourage professional help when necessary. Our corporation offers services to help employees deal with loss, divorce, and other events that occur in their personal lives.

6. Bonus: regardless of how they act, treat them with as much love and compassion as you can.

---

* Mental Health America, "Bereavement and Grief," Bereavement and Grief, accessed January 28, 2021, https://www.mhanational.org/bereavement-and-grief.

Fine Caviar

Discover and walk in your purpose.

Reflecting on life and telling these stories hasn't been easy. I've tried to think back and ask myself questions about choices I've made. At times, I have been afraid of the truth. But that's what it takes. That is the debt I owe. Examining your past helps you get clarity on your future. Reminiscing my achievements and failures, I realized that many things have guided me over the years.

One thing that guides me is this imaginary judge peeking over my shoulder. I feel that if I mess up or do wrong, then it is a blackout for my entire race. Despite my embrace of all kinds of people, I do recognize that not everyone can see me for who I am. I feel pressure to be a "credit to my race." One day, I hope that really means being a credit to the human race, but the little judge is still viewing the color of my skin. I do not want to let my race down.

As a result, I have always striven to exceed expectations. At work, I have gotten special awards, worked to solve major problems, I've done it all...because I *have* to. No matter what, though, there are people in positions of power who still stereotype and curl their lips at black people or other minorities and think we are not as smart or can't handle pressure. Perhaps, I cannot change any hearts or minds, but I feel as if I owe it to myself, and others like me, to do my best. I hope that by doing my best, I can eliminate, or at least help begin to dismantle, stereotypes and pave the way so other minorities behind me will be given a chance.

Growing up, I was told I would never be anything. That was a lie. So now, my reputation is everything to me. If my name is on it, I'm going to bust my butt, and I'm going to do all I can, so that when people walk away they say, "Oh, man, that Thomas guy is the real deal. He sticks to his word." Another thing that guides me is my reputation. If I tell you I am going to run a mile and meet you, I'm going to run a mile and meet you, even if I have to crawl that last hundred feet. My word is my number one.

All these things are also tied to my competitive nature. I feel like I must give it my all. If I start something, whether it be work, investments, or anything I am involved in, I have to give it everything I've got. That is one of the things I want to instill in my kids. I want them to do their best, not just enough to get by. You cannot control anyone or anything else but your own effort. Whatever you sign up for, you have got to put your all into it. If you do, you can go far.

Reputation, competition, and the invisible judge all guide me in some way, but the most profound driver in my life is a sense of purpose. I honestly believe that God created everyone with a purpose, and that the meaning of life is finding one's purpose and fulfilling it to your utmost. Considering where I come from and all I have endured, where I am right now and where I'm headed, there's a purpose for all of that.

I have struggled with that because I wanted to wait until some perfect moment in the future, such as after I became a millionaire or after I became super successful, to share my story.

But the more I thought about it, and considered all the kids who could benefit from my struggle, from learning about how I got from the Hood and into the upper middle class, I realized I couldn't wait. I have accomplished so much to this point, especially when I travel to Greenville and see familiar faces and witness their struggles. Some of them are barely making it.

I have made it so far already. The ups and downs have only made it easier to recognize my starting point. Here I am. I am not on the highest mountain, but I climbed this one. Here I stand, ready for the next adventure.

So I felt it was time. Time to walk in my purpose. To show my work, as any good math or engineering student would do.

FINAL REFLECTION: *What should you take away from this?*

I cannot publish this book without talking about 2020. This year has been the most challenging one in my life. We lost national symbols like Representative John Lewis (who spent most of his life fighting social injustice), Katherine Johnson (a mathematician who calculated rocket trajectories and Earth orbits for NASA's early space missions), Donald Stratton (one of the remaining USS Arizona crew members who survived the attack on Pearl Harbor), Earl Graves Sr. (one who championed black businesses as the founder of the first African-American owned magazine focusing on black entrepreneurs), Nick Cordero (a Tony Award-nominated actor who specialized in playing tough guys on Broadway in shows such as *Waitress*, *A Bronx Tale*, and *Bullets Over Broadway*), Jim Lehrer (cohost and later host of the nightly PBS *NewsHour* that, for decades, offered a thoughtful take on current events), Regis Philbin (the amiable host who shared his life with television viewers over morning coffee for decades in *Regis and Kathie Lee,* and helped himself and some fans strike it rich with the game show *Who Wants to Be a Millionaire*), and Chadwick Boseman (actor who played every black person's favorite superhero, *Black Panther*, along with a number of other famous black people).

COVID-19 has affected the world. At the time of this writing, the virus has killed nearly 400,000 Americans, more than two million worldwide. Regardless of what you believe or have been told, most of those deaths could have been prevented. COVID-19 is not the first pandemic that we have faced in my lifetime. Rather than work together, countries, leaders, governors, mayors and citizens approached the virus their own way. At first, some called it a hoax until it showed up at their backdoor. Others focused on the economy and political gain. The rest wanted to take extreme measures by shutting the country down for some unspecified time. Some people felt that social distancing and wearing a mask was a violation of their constitutional freedoms. This resulted in a lot of confusion, anger, and economic ruin for the poor and middle class. Ironically, the wealthy became even richer. Read "How billionaires saw their net worth increase by half a trillion dollars during the pandemic."* The history books are filled with stories of how the elite tend to profit from distracting, entertaining, or sending the poor to fight needless wars. If we are fighting each other over race, abortion, immigration, flags, and other distractions, we cannot see the billions of taxpayer dollars being sent to the rich, regardless of political party.

Second, the death of George Floyd brought our country to a breaking point. For over eight minutes, the world watched a white police officer pin his knee on the neck of a black man like a lion gripping the neck and the last bit of life out of a captured gazelle. The world watched this man die as the police officer showed no emotion and continued to press harder, as local observers pleaded for mercy. This event sparked protests in most cities in the United States and major cities around the world. I have seen and experienced injustice by some police officers in the past, but this event really affected me. For the next month or so, I watched the news networks like an addict, waiting for someone to step up and reunite us. Instead, I watched my government clear out protesters so that the president could get a picture of himself holding the Bible upside down in front of a church. What the hell? What do I tell my boys?

I have never seen our country as divided as we are right now. It does not help when the leader of the free world is so divisive in public, but understands the struggles in private. The world would be a better place if he would stop tweeting and let his team do their jobs, but he is not the only person at fault. The media is showing peaceful protesters one minute, then rioters and looters, and last folks calling for violence and reparations from slavery. Some people are calling every white person racist. One major news network is calling peaceful protesters, or people calling for police reform, socialists or

---

* Hiatt Woods, "How Billionaires Saw Their Net Worth Increase by Half a Trillion Dollars during the Pandemic," Business Insider (Business Insider, October 30, 2020), https://www.businessinsider.com/billionaires-net-worth-increases-coronavirus-pandemic-2020-7.

unpatriotic. The other does not miss a minute to pound the president. The president is sowing seeds of mistrust in our election system and government. My governor sued his mayor over the mask mandate. It is all overwhelming.

Who do you trust? Scan the back of your dollar bill. It reads, "In God, we trust." Never put all your trust in any human being. Before voting, research candidates with God-like qualities, such as displaying compassion for all citizens, regardless of race or political affiliation. Search for someone who seeks the greater good for humanity, even if it costs re-election, adheres to fiscal responsibility, even if it angers their base, and who has had some level of personal sacrifice, so that sending our soldiers to war is the last resort.

Let's focus on the positives. Never in my forty-five years on this earth have I seen so many people take a stand against social injustice. Lebron James, the whole Milwaukee Bucks team, Adam Silver, and the entire NBA said enough was enough and refused to play if changes were not made. Naomi Osaka withdrew from the Western and Southern Open, an event she had a great chance of winning, to protest racial injustice. Coach Dawn Staley (another one of my role models) and her talented University of South Carolina Women's basketball team shined a light on the need for racial equality in my home state by protesting during the national anthem. The WNBA and other sport leagues, including NASCAR, expressed their support and acted. Leaders from corporations, like Southern Company, voiced their concerns and engaged in difficult conversations about race with their employees, taking steps to start fixing the issues. The true leaders in our country, including all the peaceful protesters and our courageous young people, took a stand. Even some friends of mine who support our president expressed their support and wanted guidance as to what they could do to help. God has been working through all his angels on earth. And EVERY human being has the choice to be an angel for others, regardless of race, gender, religion, economic class or political party.

To keep the peace at work, I rarely discuss politics. The president has said things that some people have been thinking and wanting to say for years. It makes them feel good that they finally have a leader who shares their values, but does that make them racist? Absolutely not. Slavery was a painful period in our history and cannot be solved by giving trillions of taxpayer dollars, most likely government debt, to descendants of slaves. Instead of correcting a horrific mistake of the past by taking away dollars from future generations, let's invest that money today in improving schools, businesses, and homes in poor neighborhoods so that ALL have the opportunity to live prosperous lives if they desire. Let's provide opportunities for people to work hard to achieve their dreams. Also, let's provide second chances for people that have made bad decisions. Should society reject a person for the rest of their life for being with the wrong crowd at the wrong time or stealing a loaf of bread, as Jean Valjean did in Victor Hugo's *Les Misérables*? Take note of how many people Jean enriched after he was given a second chance by the bishop.

Most importantly, be careful about choosing sides. Perform your due diligence. Does that person or group share your values? What is their motivation? Is it for social improvement or political or economic gain? Are they associated with violence? Vote with your ballot and your currency. Do not buy from companies that do not agree with your values. Last, never respond with emotion, unless it is love, or violence. The best revenge against racists, and other haters, is for you to respond differently than they expected, and to succeed in whatever you are doing.

Always smile, even when hurt. Do your best to work harder and smarter. Be humble and hungry for knowledge from any source. Treat everyone, including your haters, like you want to be treated. For those who upset you, smile, and recite, "God, please forgive them for they know not what they do." Your haters do not know that they could be messing with the next teacher, engineer, mayor,

CEO, professional athlete, doctor, inventor, president, or other gem that you will become for our society.

I believe in you!

I pray that God blesses you more than you can imagine and that you share those blessings with others in need.

Final Thoughts

I shelved the first version of this book more than a decade ago because of fear that it wouldn't be accepted. A fear that it would be rejected due to me not being filthy rich, or the fear that my coworkers and corporation would find out that I was one of those at-risk kids who we visited from time to time. However, every day I waited, more teenagers gave up on their dreams, were misguided into believing that they are owed something, or believed that they would be outcasts their entire lives. This may have resulted in school dropouts, jail times, or death worst of all.

We can't delay any longer because the world is becoming more challenging as simple rights and freedoms are slowly removed. At a time when I am thinking that things are improving, especially with president-elect Joe Biden taking office on January 20, the presidential election results show that we have a long way to go.

This morning, I saw an older white man wearing a City of Marietta Police T-shirt with the sleeves cut off, displaying his Buffalo Bills tattoo on his right forearm. Since I grew up a Bills fan, I approached him.

"Good morning, sir," I said as I smiled and wiped the sweat from my forehead after my hour-long workout. He smiled. "Is that a Buffalo Bills tattoo or does it represent something else?" I asked.

"It is a Buffalo Bills tattoo," he replied, pausing a few minutes from his workout. He was a nice, older gentleman, probably in his early sixties, from Buffalo and had moved to Georgia to escape the cold winters.

"I have been a fan since a teen watching Jim Kelly, Thurman Thomas, Bruce Smith, Andre Reed, and James Lofton lead the team to four back-to-back Super Bowls in the early 1990s," I replied.

"I was at the Super Bowl when Scott Norwood missed the game-winning forty-seven-yard field goal." He smiled with excitement as if he had connected with a friend from New York. "But I stopped watching the NFL this year because of all the mess that's going on."

"What do you mean?" I said with disbelief. This man had tattooed the team on his arm. Most of my friends wear the fan gear and argue about who has the most Super Bowl rings, but that is it.

He paused as his smile quickly converted to sadness. "They will not talk to us. We [the police union] reached out to them to start some dialogue and work toward a solution, but they refused to talk to us."

"Times are crazy right now," I said, displaying empathy. "But you will get to watch the games again soon, hopefully."

"I hope so," he replied.

"Well, have a great day." I smiled. He greeted me with a smile then continued his workout.

As a child, I was never a fan of the police because it felt like they lived in my neighborhood. Responding to my drunk uncle pissing and cussing in the street or to my other uncle breaking into the house to steal to fulfill his crack addiction, raiding my next-door neighbor's crack house with weapons drawn while we played in the front yard, or stopping my friends on the street, thinking we were up to something not good. But I was a child and did not understand.

Over the years, I have met many police officers. One of my favorite cousins is a police officer in Anderson, South Carolina. They are great people who care about keeping the peace. When we run away from danger, they run toward it to protect us. I would venture to say that a large fraction of them served in the military, swearing an oath to protect all American citizens.

But there have been some evil events involving the police that happened recently that have affected all of us. The death of George Floyd, Breanna Taylor, Atatiana Jefferson, Stephon Clark, Botham Jean, Philando Castile, Freddie Gray, Tamir Rice, Eric Garner, and the individuals who you may know that never made national news all stirred up memories of the Rodney King beating in 1991. Anger and hate toward the police may have been your initial emotions. They were mine. But hate and anger will only lead to long-term unhappiness, if not channeled toward positive actions. Also, why hate an entire group who has sworn to protect you? We must do the following:

1. Avoid them. Do not break the law or be with anyone who will do so.

2. Respect authority. Greet him or her with "Yes, sir" or "Yes, ma'am." Hold back your emotions and answer their questions clearly.

3. Put yourself in their shoes. If you responded to a domestic abuse call last night and the husband sucker punched you, or you were shot at while responding to

a robbery, or your buddy was killed for simply wearing the uniform, then how would you approach similar calls for help? On top of that, the person who you were called to help shouts profanities and disrespect at you.

4. Work with the community and with local leaders to identify the good police officers and have the few bad apples removed from the force.

5. Always keep the dialogue open, even with people who do not see eye to eye with you.

People are inherently good. We will give our blood, sweat, and tears to defend our family, friends, coworkers, and country. We respect others who do the same, even if they are from other countries. All we ask is for a fair chance to support our families and wellbeing. Police are people. Government workers are people. Together, we are great and can overcome anything.

FINAL CAVIAR TIME

Go to your private space or find a new one. Close and lock the door. Stare at yourself in the mirror. Repeat these words:

"God, thank You for everything that You have done for my loved ones and me. We are truly blessed. Thank You for my wisdom, patience, and understanding. Thank You for continuing to grow and lead me toward my purpose.

Please continue to work through me, and all your angels on earth, to make this a better place for ALL. The world has so much potential when we put aside our differences and work together. I see it on a smaller scale when I work on expensive projects, especially those that involve teamwork across different nationalities and economic or social backgrounds.

God, thank You for all that You've done for me!"

PROFESSIONAL TIDBIT

Why am I on earth? Without government assistance, my mom could not afford to feed and clothe me. When I was a teen and contemplating suicide, why didn't God allow me to carry it out? I could not provide any value to anyone. When it appeared that society had turned its back on us, how did I survive when some of my friends didn't? My friends and I were thugs. What can I offer people? I am not a celebrity, executive, or rich.

Many people believe that their purposes arise from their special gifts and sets them apart from other people. That is only part of the truth. It also grows from their connection to others. Once they find their paths and help others achieve their dreams, they will achieve greatness.

Rick Warren's *The Purpose-Driven Life* sends the reader on a forty-day spiritual adventure to find one's purpose. In addition to reading the book, my wife and I participated in a multi-week *Purpose-Driven Life* workshop via our church. It was enlightening. We met some lifelong friends and I credit the book and workshop with helping Mel and I refine our purpose.

What is my purpose?

1. To constantly push myself, my family, and everyone around me toward greatness. Every obstacle overcome is a sign that God is in our corner.

2. To build up and celebrate people around me. Every person has a God-given gift.

3. To be a testimony to others that they can overcome anything with focus, patience, determination, and faith. God puts us through different experiences to strengthen and build us for something great that is coming next.

4. To tear down as many false stereotypes as possible. We can help God show people his greatness by giving others a chance to better themselves.

5. To build generational wealth (i.e., assets, income, knowledge, relationships, love). God want us to grow his kingdom.

When you discover your purpose, you will walk around with a joy that few can take from you. You will have a wider view of life's events. Things will appear to be easy to you. You will continue to have challenges. But your perception of them will be different.

Until We Meet Again

I hope that you have enjoyed the book, especially the Caviar Times. It was a late addition to the book. Please don't think I am crazy for what I am about to say, but I talk to myself often. My brain tends to respond when I speak words of action to it. For example, when I played high school football as the starting cornerback at Greenville High, I would try to predict the next play. If we could stop or limit the opponent's offense to three yards or less for three consecutive plays, and without receiving a penalty, then we could go chill out on the bench until the next series. During a game with Wade Hampton High, I watched the quarterback's eyes and the receiver's route as I backpedaled. "He is going to throw the ball to the receiver I am defending," I would say quietly. "Oh shoot, the ball is in the air," I would continue. "Break!" This was usually the command of my defensive backs coach to plant my foot, change direction, and sprint toward the ball. In this case, I caught an interception and nearly ran it back for a touchdown.

I did the same in the military. During physical training tests (PT), when we ran for miles and miles, I would say to myself "Push harder. It's only another mile and you have run three already." It worked. I would feel such a feeling of accomplishment at the end, because my brain and body wanted to quit.

In college, I would study for exams and quizzes and think that I was going to ace them. Then, I would be given the tests and realize that the questions were not like anything I studied. For a few minutes, I would stare hopelessly at the test or wall. Then, I would say. "I am smart. I can do this. What is the professor really asking in this question?" Lo and behold, the answer would come to me.

Others do not have to hear you talking to yourself. And no, you are not crazy. When I shared this with someone, they said that you are not crazy unless you start to answer yourself.

Always speak words of encouragement to yourself. Do it until it becomes a belief. That belief will help shape your character, and your character will lead to actions that will change your life.

BIBLIOGRAPHY

Mental Health America. Bereavement and Grief. Accessed January 28, 2021. https://www.mhanational.org/bereavement-and-grief.

Woods, Hiatt. "How Billionaires Saw Their Net Worth Increase by Half a Trillion Dollars during the Pandemic." Business Insider, October 30, 2020. https://businessinsider.com/billionaires-net-worth-increases-coronavirus-pandemic-2020-7.

Covey, Stephen R. *The 7 Habits of Highly Effective People: Powerful Lessons in Personal Change.* New York: Simon & Schuster, 1996.

Carlson, Richard. *Don't Sweat the Small Stuff.* New York: Hyperion, 1998.

Greene, Robert. *The 48 Laws of Power.* New York: Viking Penguin, 1998.

Griffith, Samuel B. *Sun Tzu: The Art of War.* New York: Oxford University Press, 1963.

Baldridge, Letitia. *New Complete Guide to Executive Manners.* New York: Rawson Associates (Simon & Schuster), 1993.

Brown, Les. *It's Not Over Until You Win: How to Become the Person You Always Wanted to Be – No Matter What the Obstacle.* New York: Simon & Schuster, 1997.

Thomas, Marlo and Phil Donahue. *What Makes a Marriage Last: 40 Celebrated Couples Share with Us the Secrets to a Happy Life.* New York: Harper Collins, 2020.

Chapman, Gary. *The 5 Love Languages: The Secret to Love That Lasts*. Chicago: Northfield Publishing, 2015.

Hill, Napolean. *Think and Grow Rich!* The Ralston Society, 1937.

Tyson, Eric. *Personal Finance for Dummies,* 2nd edition. Chicago: IDG Books Worldwide, 1997.

Tyson, Eric. *Investing for Dummies*. Chicago: IDG Books Worldwide, 1996.

Kiyosaki, Robert and Sharon L. Lechter CPA. *Rich Dad Poor Dad: What the Rich Teach Their Kids about Money That the Poor and Middle Class Do Not!* New York: Warner Books, 2000.

Jenkins, Lee. *Taking Care of Business: Establishing a Financial Legacy for the African American Family*. Chicago: Moody Publishers, 2001.

Clason, George S. *The Richest Man in Babylon*. Dauphin Publications (Clason Publishing Company), 1926.

Gurney, Dr. Karen. *Stacked: Double Your Job Interviews, Leverage Recruiters, Unlock LinkedIn*. Karen Gurney, 2017.

Warren, Rick. *The Purpose Driven Life: What on Earth Am I Here For?* Grand Rapids: Zondervan, 2002.

OTHER GREAT BOOKS IN MY LIBRARY

Teweles, Richard J. and Frank J. Jones. *The Futures Game: Who Wins, Who Loses, & Why.* New York: McGraw-Hill, 1987.

Graham, Benjamin. *The Intelligent Investor: The Definitive Book on Value Investing.* New York: Harper,1973.

Boswell, Deborah and Greg Womble. *Become a Confident Business Communicator.* Birmingham: Deborah Boswell, 2017. **The best communication coach I have ever hired!**

Grover, Tim S. and Shari Lesser Wenk. *Relentless: From Good to Great to Unstoppable.* New York: Scribner, 2014.

Clear, James. *Atomic Habits: An Easy & Proven Way to Build Good Habits & Break Bad Ones.* New York: Avery, 2018.

Coleman, Harvey J. *Empowering Yourself: The Organizational Game Revealed.* Dubuque: Kendall/Hunt Publishing, 1996.

Kiyosaki, Robert T. and Sharon L. Lechter CPA. *Rich Dad's Cashflow Quadrant: Employee, Self-Employed, Business Owner, or Investor… Which Is the Best Quadrant for You?* New York: Warner Books, 1999.

Kiyosaki, Robert T. and Sharon L. Lechter CPA. *Rich Dad's Guide to Investing: What the Rich Invest In, That the Poor and Middle Class Do Not!* New York: Warner Books, 2000.

Tyson, Eric. *Mutual Funds for Dummies,* 2nd edition. Chicago: IDG Books Worldwide, 1996.

Ramsey, Dave. *The Total Money Makeover: A Proven Plan for Financial Fitness.* Nashville: Nelson Books, 2013.

Gerber, Michael E. *The E-Myth Revisited: Why Most Small Businesses Don't Work and What to Do about It.* New York: HarperCollins, 2001.

Stanley, Thomas J. PhD and William D. Danko, PhD. *The Millionaire Next Door: The Surprising Secrets of America's Wealthy.* New York: Simon and Schuster, 1996.

Desai, Panache. *Discovering Your Soul Signature: A 33-Day Path to Purpose, Passion & Joy.* New York: Random House, 2014.

Having Fun Writing
(unedited)

My Candle

Bundled in a jar, it waits patiently for its opportunity to shine…
Until it borrows light from another to unlock its potential.
The smell of vanilla fills the room as its flame beams bright.
Twenty ounces of calm provide a soothing
atmosphere for one to reflect.
As I watch the flame flicker, I notice tears forming on the wick.
Can one burn bright without crying or sweating?
Can one be successful without producing a few
tears or beads of sweat along the way?
Uncontrolled flames cause disaster: but this one
is independent, elegant, and tranquil…
While performing well within its fragile structure.
When called upon, it has enough power to
expand your vision in the dark.
When combined with others, it can light up a large room.
When sunshine arrives, it returns to its elegance
awaiting its next opportunity to serve.

Did You Like the Book?

If so, then help us spread the word by doing these five things:

1. Leave a positive review so others will be encouraged to purchase and read the book.

2. Share the QR code below or the website (www.welfarecheesetofinecaviar.com) with a friend or loved one.

3. Share your copy of the book with someone.

4. Find ways in which you can make a difference in one person's life.

5. Continue pursuing your dreams with passion and purpose.

About the Author

Thomas Wideman was born and raised in the grip of poverty, forced to mature fast. In those critical moments, he decided to transcend his circumstances through academic achievement. Student body vice president and starting cornerback on the varsity football team, these ventures served as positive distractions from at-home struggles and leverage on college applications.

After high school, he joined the U.S. Army Reserve as a Chemical Operations Specialist. Afterwards, he graduated from the University of South Carolina with a BS in Chemical Engineering and from Georgia State University with an MBA in Finance.

His memoir, *Welfare Cheese to Fine Caviar*, shares his most transformative life experiences to help fulfill his mission of improving society one person at a time. When he isn't working, Thomas enjoys spending quality time with his wife, Melanie, a civil engineer and owner of A Little Slice of Heaven Bakery, and their sons, Isaiah and Noah.

We believe that the majority of us love our fellow human being regardless of race, gender, religion, sexual preference, or other demographic. We must resist racism and extremism at all costs.

Let's set people up for success by:

1. Providing them the opportunities and tools to achieve their goals
2. Helping and encouraging them to learn from their failures.
3. Celebrating their accomplishments.

Regardless of our political affiliations, let's all work on bringing our country back to the center where healthy debate and compromise leads to prosperous lives for everyone.

Currently, we are a small organization that sells motivational products (books, posters, shirts, etc.). However, our goal is to help the less fortunate pave successful paths in the world.

www.ingramcontent.com/pod-product-compliance
Lightning Source LLC
Chambersburg PA
CBHW070900080526
44589CB00013B/1148